yellow face

yellow face

DAVID HENRY HWANG

FOREWORD BY Frank Rich

THEATRE COMMUNICATIONS GROUP
NEW YORK
2009

Yellow Face is published by Theatre Communications Group, Inc., 520 Eighth Avenue, 24th Floor, New York, NY 10018-4156

"Shall We Dance?" music by Richard Rodgers, words by Oscar Hammerstein II, is used by special arrangement with The Rodgers & Hammerstein Organization, www.rnh.com.

This publication is made possible in part with public funds from the New York State Council on the Arts, a State Agency.

TCG books are exclusively distributed to the book trade by Consortium Book Sales and Distribution.

Library of Congress Cataloging-in-Publication Data

Hwang, David Henry, 1957–
Yellow face / David Henry Hwang.
p. cm.
ISBN 978-1-55936-340-2
1. Identity (Psychology)—Drama. I. Title.
PS3558.W83Y45 2008
812'.54—dc22
2009028208
CIP

Cover, book design and composition by Lisa Govan
Cover image by The Public Theater
Author photo courtesy of the author

First Edition, September 2009
Sixth Printing, January 2023

Acknowledgments

Special thanks to Pannill Camp, my tireless researcher, as well as all my sources, who so generously contributed to this play, including those who do not appear in it: Jack Shafer, Jeff Yang, the *New York Times* investigative reporter who spoke to me on condition of anonymity, Alice Young, Frank H. Wu, Wayman Wong and Nicholas Hytner. The Dong musical selections are taken from *Dong Folk Songs: People and Nature in Harmony*; thanks to Joanna C. Lee, Ken Smith and Lee Wai Kit for permission. I also want to acknowledge and give special thanks to Margaret Cho for an excerpt from "I'm the One That I Want," copyright © 2000 by Cho Taussig Productions, 2001 by Margaret Cho.

Foreword

By Frank Rich

As we look at David Henry Hwang's brilliant career from the vantage point of the new American era of Obama, it's more clear than ever that he has always been ahead of the curve. Though inevitably labeled an Asian American writer, Hwang has actually been among the quintessential American playwrights, period, of his time. In his work, ethnic, racial and sexual identities are fluid, and the cultures that stir within the American melting pot alternately do battle and cross-pollinate. Near the end of *Yellow Face*, the play's protagonist, the playwright DHH, confesses an ambition "to take words like 'Asian' and 'American,' like 'race' and 'nation,'" and "mess them up so bad no one has any idea what they even mean anymore." And so Hwang has done exactly that—and not just in this particular play. If there's a repeated refrain to the drama and farce that mark his work, it's that the multicultural categories that have so long both defined and divided America inexorably coalesce into an uncategorizable but universal humanity. America's new and unlikely president has called himself a "mutt," and so are most of Hwang's American characters. Those mutts can speak for many of us in the audience—whatever the particular multi-identities we represent within the infinite mix that is the U.S. of A.

Yellow Face is a particularly remarkable achievement, a Pirandellian comedy built out of a trio of sour real-life events from the last decade of the twentieth century: the uproar by Asian American theater artists over the casting of a white actor, Jonathan Pryce, in the starring role of a Vietnamese pimp in the big-budget Broadway musical *Miss Saigon* in 1990; the ignominious failure of Hwang's *Face Value*, a play about the *Miss Saigon* flap that closed during previews on Broadway in 1993; and a "yellow peril" hysteria of sorts that erupted in the political arena at the end of the 1990s. That's when Wen Ho Lee, a nuclear scientist in Los Alamos, was accused of espionage and, concurrently, Asian American political contributors, including Hwang's own father, the Los Angeles banker Henry Y. Hwang, were dragged into the Washington witchhunts targeting Bill Clinton. Both Wen Ho Lee and Henry Hwang, as it happened, were the subject of overheated journalistic investigations in the *New York Times*, mordantly dramatized here, that ate up many columns of newsprint to no just end. Lee was incarcerated for nine months in solitary confinement while awaiting trial, only to plead guilty to a minor charge; the judge in the case apologized to him for the prosecutorial overkill, and later Lee would receive $1,645,000 to settle a lawsuit he brought against the federal government for invasion of privacy. Henry Hwang was never charged with anything by the Washington investigators looking for Clinton campaign-finance improprieties, but along the way they, like the *Times*, tarnished his name—and face.

You'd think these circumstances would propel David Henry Hwang to write an angry, bitter play. But *Yellow Face* is all the more powerful for grasping the absurdity of the real-life events and refracting them through this writer's piquant comic vision. No character more epitomizes Hwang's buoyant tone than the poignant and at times uproarious characterization of HYH—the play's stand in for his real-life father. HYH, who arrived in America from Shanghai in the late 1940s, is head-over-heels in love with the country where he started with nothing and built a fortune. He channels Frank Sinatra's "My Way," wears Armani, delights in barking into a speakerphone and is enthralled with every last accoutrement of success. He's so loyal toward his adopted country that, as his son puts it, he's the only person who ever "went in for an IRS audit and came out with a bigger refund."

Only in America could a man like HYH seriously propose starting an organization called "Chinese Republican Bankers for

Clinton" and dream that it would pay off with the ambassadorship to Great Britain. When, instead, he gets unjustly hauled before a congressional committee (for a potpourri of accusations including "money-laundering, violation of campaign finance laws, aiding a foreign power, possibly even complicity in espionage"), he still has trouble shedding his fundamental American faith. He sees himself as a hero on national television: "Lights, cameras, senators—and me, giving it to those guys. 'You—you discriminate against Asians! This sort of thing—must never happen in America.'" He wonders out loud: "What does Ollie North have that I don't?" Perhaps the congressional investigation will even be a stepping stone to the governorship of California.

When HYH is ultimately disabused of his innocence—realizing that the system doesn't always play fair and that real life in America does not necessarily imitate the Jimmy Stewart movies he loved as a child in China—it is a grievous and moving turn of events. Yet it's not Hwang's final word. As a counterpoint to the painful chronicle of HYH's disillusionment, the playwright comes up with one of his most ingenious fictional characters: Marcus G. Dahlman, aka Marcus Gee, a young actor whose Off-Off-Off Broadway appearance as a Japanese American soldier in a play at the Marin Community Center leads DHH to cast him as an Asian American in his ill-fated play *Face Value*.

Marcus looks white and is white. But, as DHH says at one point, "nowadays, it's so hard to tell." The freak Marin community theater casting mixup, Equity rules and the niceties of political correctness allow Marcus to keep passing for part-Asian—indeed to become something of a paragon of Asian American success—to the absurd extreme that he can star as the King of Siam in a touring production of *The King and I*. (Let us not forget that the Broadway originator of that classic Asian role, Yul Brynner, was, like Hwang's fictional Marcus, of Russian ancestry. We should also note that another Rodgers & Hammerstein Asian-themed musical—*Flower Drum Song*—cast a white actor in a principal Chinese American role in its original Broadway production of 1958, a lapse corrected in the 2002 Broadway revival for which Hwang wrote the revised book.)

Might Marcus's perverse self-invention be a vindication of HYH's American Dream after all? "Look at me," Marcus tells DHH, "I imagined myself as something completely different from what I was," and painstakingly constructed that new identity "through sheer will and determination," just like the self-made tycoon HYH.

This case of mistaken identity takes the famous gender switch of *M. Butterfly* to a whole new level of thematic ingenuity. It also allows Hwang, who served in fact as a public face in the Equity battle against the "yellow face" casting of *Miss Saigon*, to reopen that case and upend all its various issues. (It also allows him to reopen his cultural examination of *Madama Butterfly*.) As *Yellow Face* suggests, perhaps we really do not know what "Asian" and "American" mean anymore. "It's a new world out there," says DHH. "The demographics of this country are changing so fast—and sometimes we think it's only white people who gotta adjust. But *we've* gotta start thinking differently, too."

None of this new thinking can rescue a Henry Hwang or Wen Ho Lee from being branded as "evil foreigners" when America is hungry for scapegoats. As Hwang reminds us near the end of the play, the turn-of-the-century vilification of China that abruptly halted when America discovered the virulence of a different foreign villain on Sept. 11, 2001, could return at any time in the new century. Barack Obama's elevation to the American presidency isn't the final curtain on anti-black racism either.

And yet Hwang's play—written before most Americans had heard of Obama—was prescient about an unquestionable change in our culture before others could articulate it. If I could create a dream repertory theater, it would produce all of Hwang's plays from the precocious start of his career in the early 1980s, when he was still in his twenties. Even in his earliest works—plays like *FOB.*, *The Dance and the Railroad* and *Family Devotions*—he was sending East and West into inspired cultural, philosophical and racial collisions, juxtaposing the conventions of Chinese opera with the American sitcom, Asian gods with Christianity, Chinese antiquity with Beverly Hills consumerism, unassimilated immigrants fresh off the boat with converts to all-American capitalism like HYH. Hwang's plays, like August Wilson's cycle, collectively chart the ever-changing definition of what it is to be an "American" during the fast-paced century in which our country started struggling in earnest to make its democratic ideals into a reality. That definition is still evolving, and perhaps will always be a work-in-progress. Meanwhile, *Yellow Face* is yet another example of how David Henry Hwang's art has illuminated and anticipated our ongoing national story with a sensibility unlike any other in the American theater.

yellow face

Production History

Yellow Face was originally developed at the Lark Play Development Center in New York City and subsequently developed in collaboration with the Stanford Institute for Creativity in the Arts at Stanford University. The world premiere was presented at Los Angeles's Center Theatre Group/Mark Taper Forum (Michael Ritchie, Artistic Director; Charles Dillingham, Managing Director) in association with East West Players (Tim Dang, Producing Artistic Director) and New York City's Public Theater (Oskar Eustis, Artistic Director; Mara Manus, Executive Director) in May 2007. The production was directed by Leigh Silverman; the set design was by David Korins, the costume design was by Myung Hee Cho, the lighting design was by Donald Holder and the sound design was by Darron L West; the production stage manager was James T. McDermott and the stage manager was Elizabeth Atkinson. The cast was:

DHH	Hoon Lee
MARCUS	Peter Scanavino
HYH AND OTHERS	Tzi Ma
LEAH AND OTHERS	Julienne Hanzelka Kim
THE ANNOUNCER AND NWOAOC	Anthony Torn
STUART OSTROW, ROCCO PALMIERI AND OTHERS	Lucas Caleb Rooney
JANE KRAKOWSKI, MILES NEWMAN AND OTHERS	Kathryn A. Layng

This production transferred to the Public Theater in December 2007 with the following changes: the assistant to the author was Tom Diggs, the production stage manager was Cole P. Bonenberger and the stage manager was Rebecca Goldstein-Glaze. The cast changes were:

MARCUS	Noah Bean
HYH AND OTHERS	Francis Jue

Characters

The following represents one possible assignment of actors to characters. Other combinations, involving more or fewer actors, might also be devised.

DHH

MARCUS G. DAHLMAN, aka Marcus Gee

HYH AND OTHERS: BD Wong; Bernard Jacobs; *New York Post*; Joseph Papp; *Pravda*; Rodney Hatamiya; *Boston Globe*, January 1, 1993; *Boston Globe*, February 15, 1993; Michael Riedel; Student #1; Margaret Cho; Senator Bennett; Representative DeLay; Wen Ho Lee; Protester

LEAH ANNE CHO AND OTHERS: Frank Chin; *New York Times*, July 13, 1990; *Washington Post*, August 9, 1990; B'nai B'rith; *National Review*; Carla Chang; *New York Times*, August 17, 1990; Linda; *Boston Globe*, January 1, 1993; *Boston Phoenix* #1; Gish Jen; Student #2; Margaret Fung; Don Mihail; Reporter #1; Fred Thompson; Yellowgurl8; OCC

THE ANNOUNCER; NAME WITHHELD ON ADVICE OF COUNSEL (NWOAOC)

STUART OSTROW, ROCCO PALMIERI AND OTHERS: Senator John Kerry; Cameron Mackintosh; Frank Rich; Dick Cavett; *New York Times*, August 8, 1990; *New York Times*, October 23, 1992; Mark Linn-Baker; *Christian Science Monitor*; *Boston Phoenix* #2; Bookstore Owner; William Craver; Student #4; Associated Press, March 15, 1993; *Los Angeles Times*; *Variety,*

April 27, 1996; *USA Today*, July 9, 1997; Senator Brownback; FBI Agent; Protester #1; Dr. Pichorak

JANE KRAKOWSKI, MILES NEWMAN AND OTHERS: Lily Tomlin; Vinnie Liff; *New York Times*, August 8, 1990; *New York Times*, August 17, 1990; *New York Daily News*; George F. Will; Ed Koch; *TheaterWeek*; *New York Times*, February 26, 1993; Student #3; Beatrice Chang; Fritz Friedman; Julia Dahlman; *New York Times*, September 12, 1997; Senator Shelby; Representative Jack Kingston; Protester; Senator Domenici; Dorothy Hwang; OCC Regional Director; Judge James Parker

Setting

1990 to the present. New York City; Los Angeles; Washington, D.C.; Boston; San Francisco; the Guizhou Province, China.

Note

A standard ellipses (. . .) indicates a pause or hesitation as in any play; an underlined ellipses (. . .) denotes a deletion within a quotation.

Act One

Darkness. We hear the Dong people singing Track #2 from the CD Dong Folk Songs: People and Nature in Harmony: *"We Close the Village for Rituals." Lights come up on the actors, who remain seated onstage when not playing their parts.*

DHH: E-mail, received January 30, 2006, from Marcus G. Dahlman to David Henry Hwang:

MARCUS: David, you won't believe where I am. In China. Guizhou Province, to be exact. After everything that happened in the States, I needed to take some time off. So I came to China, hoping to find—something real, true? I'm not even sure. All I know is, my life back home, it used to have purpose, a direction I really believed in—but I lost all that. *(Pause)* One night in Shanghai, a city so futuristic it makes *Blade Runner* look quaint, another "waiguoren"—another "foreigner"—told me where I could find "the soul of China." He described this amazing village he'd just visited, and a minority tribe called the Dong. *(Pause)* I flew to the provincial capital of Guiyang, then traveled ten hours by bus over roads barely paved—potholes the size of phone booths. As we climbed upwards, rice fields appeared everywhere—terraces, carved into the mountainside, centuries ago. Finally I arrived at a village called Zhencong. Soon as I stepped off

the bus, I heard a song. The Dong call their music "da ge"—
the "big song"—melodies that can only be sung by the whole
village—together. The Dong have a saying, "Rice feeds the
body, but song feeds the heart."

(Music out.)

DHH: That was the first of Marcus's e-mails to me. More than a
few Asian Americans still wonder what happened to him. In
mainstream culture, however, Marcus, like most Asian
American celebrities, remains virtually unknown. True, at
the time of his downfall, a few took note.

THE ANNOUNCER: Senator John Kerry:

SENATOR JOHN KERRY: It's hardened people's cynicism. Everyone loses for that.

DHH: But for the most part, the story of a minor figure in a couple of discredited scandals disappeared after one or two
press cycles. Blink and you would've missed it. As for my
own role in the story, some Asian Americans noticed, but
they chose to forgive me for my mistakes.

THE ANNOUNCER: Playwright Frank Chin:

FRANK CHIN: David Henry Hwang is a white racist asshole.

DHH: Well, most of them did, anyway. After all, I was a respected
figure in the community, the first Asian playwright to have a
play produced on Broadway. I even appeared on national
television—with Lily Tomlin!

(Awards ceremony entrance music.)

LILY TOMLIN: And the 1988 Tony Award for Best Play goes
to . . . *M. Butterfly.* Author: David Henry Hwang. Producers:
Stuart Ostrow and David Geffen.

("Un Bel Di" music from Madama Butterfly.*)*

DHH: From Mickey Rooney playing Japanese in *Breakfast at
Tiffany's* to Bruce Lee being passed over in favor of David
Carradine for a TV series called *Kung Fu*, Asians have con-
sistently been caricatured, denied the right even to play ourselves. Well, it's a new day in America. We're entering the
1990s, and all that stops now!

(The sound of a ringing phone. Music out.)

Hello?

BD: Hi, David, it's BD.

THE ANNOUNCER: BD Wong, Tony Award–winning star of *M. Butterfly.* June 25, 1990.

DHH: Hey, Bradd, what's up?

BD: You heard about this whole *Miss Saigon* business?

DHH: You mean, the musical? In London?

BD: Jonathan Pryce is playing an Asian pimp.

DHH: Yeah, Roz Chao saw it there. Said his eyes are all taped up and everything. That would never happen here.

BD: They're bringing the show to Broadway.

DHH: I know. But this is America—they're not gonna cast a white guy here.

BD: They have.

DHH: You're sure the actor's white? Maybe he's mixed race. Nowadays, it's so hard to tell. He could have a Caucasian father, so his last name wouldn't sound Asian or maybe he's one of those Korean adoptees, or—

BD: David, it's Jonathan Pryce. *(Pause)* The producer's saying they conducted this worldwide talent search, and they couldn't find any Asian qualified to play the part.

DHH: They can't do that.

BD: That's what a lot of us think.

DHH: Yellow face? In this day and age? It's—it's—did someone suddenly turn the clock back to 1920? Are we all going to smear shoe polish on our faces, and start singing "Mammy"?

BD: We thought if you'd be willing to write a letter—

DHH: You bet I will. Trust me, they won't get away with it.

(Sound of keys tapping on an IBM Selectric.)

Dear Actors' Equity:

THE ANNOUNCER: The national union for stage actors.

DHH: I learned some news today, which left me feeling surprised and dismayed . . .

THE ANNOUNCER: *New York Times,* July 13, 1990:

NEW YORK TIMES, JULY 13, 1990: *Miss Saigon* casting protested. Asian American[s] **. . .** [have complained about] the casting

of a Caucasian in one of the show's principal [Asian] roles
... David Henry Hwang, the Tony Award–winning playwright of *M. Butterfly*, registered his protest ... in a letter
sent to Actors' Equity.

DHH: I had dared to suppose that the yellow face days of Charlie
Chan and Fu Manchu had been relegated forever to the clos-
ets of historical kitsch ... Mr. Pryce is an excellent actor, but
I would be equally upset were he cast as [an African Amer-
ican character like] Boy Willie in [August Wilson's play] *The
Piano Lesson.*

THE ANNOUNCER: Cameron Mackintosh, producer of *Miss
Saigon*:

CAMERON MACKINTOSH: This is a tempest in an Oriental
teapot.

DHH *(To the audience)*: Actors' Equity union took my side in the
casting dispute and arranged a meeting with the *Miss Saigon*
team, including producer Cameron Mackintosh.

CAMERON MACKINTOSH: The gall of it, the sheer hypocrisy!
This is all because BD Wong wants a job, isn't it? And the
fact that you have made a public spectacle of the issue—I
don't believe we can work any longer in this atmosphere.
How can you support such a blatant restriction of artistic
freedom?

THE ANNOUNCER: Vinnie Liff, casting director, *Miss Saigon*:

VINNIE LIFF: David, if you know any Asian actor who'd be right
for that part—forty to fifty years old, classical training,
worldwide stature—please, give me his name. We have
searched literally around the world.

DHH: Actually, I called John Lone.

THE ANNOUNCER: Star of *The Last Emperor*.

DHH: He said his manager had contacted your office to say he
was interested in the part, but no one ever called them back.

THE ANNOUNCER: Bernard Jacobs, president of the Shubert
Theatres:

BERNARD JACOBS: This man is trying to stir up trouble. That's
why you sent that letter of yours to the papers.

DHH: No, I—

CAMERON MACKINTOSH: If you were really seeking to do something constructive, why would you have turned this into a
circus?

BERNARD JACOBS: You sent your letter to that reporter. To stir up trouble.

DHH: No, I—didn't.

BERNARD JACOBS: Now you're lying. This man is a liar. I don't know why we're even listening to him.

CAMERON MACKINTOSH: The atmosphere is poisoned. Unless conditions improve, I don't see how I can bring this show into New York.

THE ANNOUNCER: *New York Times*, August 8, 1990:

NEW YORK TIMES, AUGUST 8, 1990: [Actors' Equity] union bars white in Asian role.

THE ANNOUNCER: *Washington Post*, August 9:

WASHINGTON POST, AUGUST 9, 1990: The Broadway production of *Miss Saigon* ... has been canceled, producer Cameron Mackintosh announced today.

DHH: It has certainly never been my intention to see a show canceled. I simply felt that an important point had to be made, and this has clearly been achieved.

THE ANNOUNCER: *New York Times:*

NEW YORK TIMES, AUGUST 8, 1990: Last night, Equity ... received a petition from one hundred and fifty of its members ... to reconsider its decision.

THE ANNOUNCER: *New York Post:*

NEW YORK POST: Asian American and other protesters demonstrated yesterday in Times Square, demanding that Equity stick to its decision.

THE ANNOUNCER: *The Daily News:*

NEW YORK DAILY NEWS: Yesterday, a scuffle between opposing camps in the *Miss Saigon* dispute broke out in the lobby of Actors' Equity's offices. Pressure is mounting on Actors' Equity.

THE ANNOUNCER: The Anti-Defamation League of B'nai B'rith:

B'NAI B'RITH: Casting decisions should be based on individual talent and merit, not on race or—

THE ANNOUNCER: Columnist George F. Will:

GEORGE F. WILL: The trendy racism of Actors' Equity—

THE ANNOUNCER: Frank Rich, chief drama critic, *New York Times:*

FRANK RICH: Jonathan Pryce's brilliant performance is as essential to *Miss Saigon* as Joel Grey's was to *Cabaret*. Maybe even more—

THE ANNOUNCER: Producer Joseph Papp:

JOSEPH PAPP: As a producer, I have concerns about anyone imposing conditions, but as a citizen . . . I think Equity did the proper and heroic—

THE ANNOUNCER: *The National Review:*

NATIONAL REVIEW: "Producer"? "Citizen"? As if the two states of being were somehow disconnected?

THE ANNOUNCER: Former New York mayor Ed Koch:

ED KOCH: Now it's Actors' Equity, playing the censor!

THE ANNOUNCER: Talk show host Dick Cavett:

DICK CAVETT: The bonehead decision of the year.

THE ANNOUNCER: *Pravda:*

PRAVDA: SLUchai *Miss Saigon* demonstRIruyet, kak Ameri-KANskaye OBschestva praktiKUyet tsenZUru.

(The "beep" of a phone answering machine.)

CARLA CHANG: David, it's Carla Chang.

THE ANNOUNCER: Asian American actress and political activist.

CARLA CHANG: I've already left a couple of messages. We need you down at Actors' Equity's offices at noon tomorrow to—

(DHH picks up.)

DHH: Carla, it's David.

CARLA CHANG: Screening calls?

DHH: No! No, just washing my hair.

CARLA CHANG: Equity council is meeting tomorrow to reconsider their decision. We're holding a rally at noon. You come down, we'll give you a placard, the press will take a few pictures—

DHH: Carla, I—don't think I can make it.

CARLA CHANG: What do you mean? Equity's under a lot of pressure. Everyone else wants them to cave, let Jonathan Pryce do the part—we need to stand up for Equity and make sure they stick to their guns.

DHH: I feel we've made our point, and now—

CARLA CHANG: And now we have a chance to stop yellow face forever!

DHH: But the artistic freedom thing—between you and me, I think this is starting to make us—look bad.

CARLA CHANG: "Look bad"? This is our Rosa Parks moment! Now, tomorrow, we need you to—

DHH: Why? Why do you need me?

CARLA CHANG: Because—you're a name the papers know and—

DHH: That's right, it's *my* name out there. *My* face in the papers—the poster child for political correctness.

CARLA CHANG: Hey, I wish it were mine.

DHH: I can't make the rally, okay? This thing will end—however it's going to end—

CARLA CHANG: David, you can't give up now!

DHH: I am not giving up! I'm doing what I think is best. For the cause.

THE ANNOUNCER: *New York Times*, August 17, 1990:

NEW YORK TIMES, AUGUST 17, 1990: [Actors' Equity] union reverses *Saigon* vote and welcomes English star.

(The sound of a ringing telephone.)

DHH: Hello.

HYH: Dave?

DHH: Hi Dad.

HYH: Wait a second— *(His voice filters into an echo effect with feedback)* There!

DHH: What happened to the connection?

HYH: I'm using my new speakerphone.

DHH: Well, it sounds like crap.

HYH: What?

DHH: I said, it sounds like—

HYH: Could you speak up? It's hard to hear over this thing.

DHH: Then pick up the receiver!

HYH: I'll turn up the volume. *(The feedback cranks up)*

DHH: Aaaah!

HYH: Your mother—

DHH: Just pick up the phone!

HYH: She didn't teach me how to work this thing.

DHH: Pick up the phone!

HYH: But that would turn off my speakerphone.

DHH: Your speakerphone is shit!

HYH: Why you have to talk like that?

(HYH picks up the phone. The sound effect goes out.)

You're right. That speakerphone is shit.

DHH: Dad, I'm a little busy right now.

HYH: Doing what?

DHH: Trying to write a new play.

HYH: Good idea.

DHH: What's that supposed to mean?

HYH: I said it was a good idea.

DHH: It's only been three years since *M. Butterfly.*

HYH: But you been smart. Keeping your name in the newspapers. That's good, Son.

DHH: You mean all that *Miss Saigon* stuff? Thank god, it's finally starting to die down.

HYH: But so many articles on you. Free publicity!

DHH: But everyone disagreed with me!

HYH: Everyone! All the big-shot guys: Dick Cavett! Ed Koch! Here, wait, this one my favorite.

DHH: You saved the articles?

HYH: "I am ashamed of my union, Actors' Equity!"

DHH: Oh, yeah—Charlton Heston.

HYH: When I was working in a laundry, could I ever have dreamed? That one day Charlton Heston would write— about *my* son? I'm telling you, this is the land of opportunity. And that *Miss Saigon*—such a big hit.

DHH: Don't remind me, okay?

HYH: Looks so beautiful. All those girls—classy.

DHH: They're half naked! Playing prostitutes!

HYH: But they're classy prostitutes.

DHH: You haven't even seen the show!

HYH: But I saw pictures in the newspaper. That producer— what's his name?

DHH: Cameron Mackintosh.

HYH: He talks about the musical—so beautiful!—a young Vietnamese girl who gives up her baby to find a better life in America.

DHH: Actually, she dies.

HYH: What?

DHH: The girl—she kills herself. It's her baby who finds a better life in America.

HYH: That's even more beautiful!

DHH: It's *Madame Butterfly* set in Vietnam.

HYH: Dave, you should do something like that. Is that what your new play is about? *Madame Butterfly* set in Vietnam?

DHH: How could I possibly—it's already been done!

HYH: See, I'm just so ignorant about these things.

DHH: Besides, I already wrote a play criticizing *Madame Butterfly*!

HYH: What play was that?

DHH: *M. Butterfly*!

HYH: Oh, right, right. You know, your *M. Butterfly*—that play is a little weird.

DHH: We've been over this.

HYH: When I come to New York next month, can you get me some tickets?

DHH: To *M. Butterfly*? It closed last year!

HYH: No, no—*Miss Saigon*!

DHH: I can't believe—

HYH: My good friend Dick Buttress, vice chairman of United California Bank, he told me he was in New York last month, and he couldn't even get a ticket! I told him, next time you go, ask my son.

DHH: What?

HYH: I told him, my son, he knows the producer, they're good friends, he worked on the show.

DHH: Dad, I protested the show!

HYH: What's the difference? That McEnroe—

DHH: Mackintosh.

HYH: Mackintosh. He knows how much you've done for his show, and I'll tell you something: he's grateful to you.

DHH: Fine. I'll get you tickets. I'll get your friend tickets. Anyone you know who can't get into *Miss Saigon*, just have them give me a call.

HYH: Thanks, Son. But not right now.

DHH: Why not?

HYH: Because you're working.

DHH: I'm trying.

HYH: What are you writing about?

DHH: Nothing.

HYH: Your father's just curious.

DHH: It's about Rudyard Kipling, okay? *(Pause)* The guy who wrote *The Jungle Book*? Kipling? I'm working on a play that deconstructs his life and work. *(Pause)* Dad?

HYH: I'll tell you the thing about *Miss Saigon*. You wanna know why it's such a big hit?

DHH: Not really.

HYH: Because it's real.

DHH: A Vietnamese prostitute falls in love with some white soldier and kills herself so her baby can come to America?

HYH: Things like that happen all the time.

DHH: How can you say—?

HYH: You don't know how much people want to come to America. I see that girl, and I think—she's like me.

DHH: You killed yourself?

HYH: No, but I would've. That's how much I wanted to come here. Even when I didn't know anything more about America than I saw in Shanghai at the movies—even then, I knew my real life wasn't the one I was living in China. Second son of a cheapskate father, who didn't even know how to talk to his children. I knew that was a fake life, and my real life was here. All those movie stars—Humphrey Bogart and Clark Gable and Frank Sinatra—they were the real me. So when I finally got here, I kept on pushing. Until one day, after I started the bank and it became a success, I looked around, at my office on the thirty-ninth floor, my house the swankiest part of San Marino, my Mercedes, my kids all in top colleges—and I thought, now, I am finally living my real life—here in America. *(Pause)* That's why the girl kills herself. Because when you can see your real life, and it's someplace else, then what's the point? If you lose hope you'll ever get there, then even if you kill yourself, it makes no difference.

DHH: Dad, I gotta go.

HYH: Sure, Son. But why?

DHH: I think I know what I want to write about.

HYH: Something besides that *Jungle Book* guy?

DHH: Yeah.

HYH: Good!

(Typing on a computer keyboard.)

THE ANNOUNCER: *TheaterWeek* magazine, September 1992:

THEATERWEEK: Take a look at the face on the cover of this magazine. Is he Chinese American, Asian American, plain American? Or someone in yellow face? Does any of this matter? These are some of the questions raised in David Henry Hwang's new farce *Face Value*.

DHH: Is race a construct which is still useful or is it mythological?

THE ANNOUNCER: *New York Times*, October 23, 1992:

NEW YORK TIMES, OCTOBER 23, 1992: The new play, which Mr. Hwang described as:

DHH: A comedy of mistaken racial identity—

NEW YORK TIMES, OCTOBER 23, 1992: —was inspired by the fracas over the casting of Jonathan Pryce as a Eurasian pimp in *Miss Saigon*.

DHH: It's a backstage farce about a musical in which the lead actor is a Caucasian playing an Asian. On opening night, two Asian American protesters sneak in to disrupt the show—dressed in white face.

THE ANNOUNCER: July 10, 1992. Auditions for *Face Value*. Present are:

STUART: Stuart Ostrow, producer of *Face Value*.

NEWMAN: Miles Newman, casting director.

RODNEY: Rodney Hatamiya, auditioning.

LINDA: Linda, reader.

RODNEY *(Reading as Randall)*: He stole my job!

LINDA *(Reading)*: He stole all our jobs!

RODNEY *(Reading as Randall)*: I really know I could've brought some truth to that role.

LINDA *(Reading)*: In this day and age—a Caucasian—playing a Chinese! And in that horrible musical! It's racist, sexist, imperialist, misogynist—

RODNEY *(Reading as Randall)*: And I didn't even get an audition.

LINDA *(Reading)*: Neither did I. Damn them!

STUART: Thank you.

DHH: That was really great, fantastic, what an audition! Thank you so much!

(Linda and Rodney exit the audition room.)

He's not right, either. There's gotta be more Asian male actors out there.

STUART: How about BD?

DHH: I just don't—I don't see BD in this one. This is our chance. To make some fresh Asian face into a Broadway star. For *M. Butterfly* we were looking for a Chinese transvestite who could sing and dance! And we found lots of them!

STUART: Yes we did.

DHH: So why is this so much harder? All we're looking for is a straight, masculine, Asian leading man.

STUART: I'll tell Miles to keep looking.

DHH: Tell him—there are hundreds of masculine Asian leading men out there. Dozens!

STUART: He keeps asking if you know any.

DHH: Is that my job? Tell him to scour the country! Somewhere out there, our star is waiting for us to find him!

THE ANNOUNCER: A performance of the play *Go for Broke*. At the Marin Community Center, California. Starring—

RODNEY: Rodney Hatamiya.

MARCUS: And Marcus G. Dahlman.

(Stage sound effects of gun battle.)

The Lost Battalion, 36th Infantry Division. From the Lone Star State.

RODNEY: They're trapped?

MARCUS: Pinned down. Krauts on all sides. *(Pause)* Look, I'm not gonna lie to you boys. It's a suicide mission, to call it anything else would be a damn lie.

RODNEY: Lieutenant Grayson, I'm not sure I can do this.

MARCUS: Listen up, Sergeant Watanabe. Do it for your country.

RODNEY: America? Where I'll always be a foreigner? Even before the war, people would ask me, "Where are you from?" And I'd tell 'em, "Stockton, California." Then they'd say, "No. Where are you *really* from?" And now, to them—I'm just another enemy Jap.

MARCUS: All right, then—do it for your family.

RODNEY: My family? Rounded up by the U.S. government and thrown behind barbed wire?

MARCUS: Sergeant, let's talk turkey. When headquarters first assigned me to an all–Japanese American battalion, I was a typical Texan—thinkin' all you boys were the enemy. But now—I've never met a finer group of Americans.

RODNEY: You're right, this is the best chance we're ever gonna get to show the world we're loyal Americans. My parents' generation—the issei—they have a saying: "Shikata ga nai." *(Off Marcus's look)* It means, "Can't be helped." "Nothing to be done."

MARCUS: Well, then, "Shikata ga nai" to you too. So—ready, boys? Charge!

RODNEY: Go for broke!

(The sounds of battle fade up, then cross-fade to audience applause.)

NEWMAN: A friend who lived in Marin sent me a newspaper article about this new show *Go for Broke.*

THE ANNOUNCER: Miles Newman, casting director, *Face Value*:

NEWMAN: It was an Asian American play—with a cast of two. One of the actors—Rodney Hatamiya—we'd already auditioned him. But the other guy—Marcus G. Dahlman—sure, his name didn't sound Asian, but as you well know, that doesn't mean anything nowadays. And this was December. Rehearsals for *Face Value* were supposed to start in three weeks, and we still hadn't found an actor for our lead Asian role. *(Pause)* The producers agreed to fly Marcus out between Christmas and New Year's for an audition.

(Marcus rises, shakes hands with Newman.)

My first thought when Marcus walked in was, "Well, it's obvious he's not one hundred percent Asian." Because of Equity rules, you can't just come out and ask an actor his race. That would be illegal—and racist. But over the years, I'd become pretty good at getting to the truth of an actor's ethnicity. *(To Marcus)* So, Marcus, where are you from?

MARCUS: Actually, I was born in Seattle.

NEWMAN: Seattle. Very . . . diverse town, isn't it?

MARCUS: Sure. You know the place?

NEWMAN: I'm so impressed by the vitality of the Asian community there.

MARCUS: It's great.

NEWMAN: Cherry Blossom Festival, Chinese New Year's Parade—you know?

MARCUS: Sure.

NEWMAN: So you've been?

MARCUS: Yeah, as a kid.

NEWMAN: The Filipino community—they must have some big annual—of their own, right? I'm so ignorant, I wish I knew—

MARCUS: Sorry, I can't—

NEWMAN: Or the Indians! Do they have any—? Or how 'bout the Vietnamese? Koreans? Hmong?

MARCUS: I'm not sure what you're—

NEWMAN: You don't happen to speak any foreign languages, do you?

MARCUS: Is one needed for the part?

NEWMAN: No, I was just—

MARCUS: Good, cuz I'm still struggling with English.

NEWMAN: Really.

MARCUS: Huh? No, I was making a—

NEWMAN: —a joke, of course.

MARCUS: Not very—

NEWMAN: I got it, I got it! —See, Marcus, I like to be direct.

MARCUS: Okay.

NEWMAN: We are—how should I put this? Oh god—we are looking to cast this role with an Asian.

MARCUS: As you should.

NEWMAN: So that's . . . all right with you?

MARCUS: Well, my background is so mixed-up, it's hard to keep track. My father is Jewish and, you know, there're some people who believe that the Lost Tribe of Israel wound up in China. *(Laughs)*

(Newman is unimpressed.)

No. Actually, I spent a lot of time in the International District with the issei, the nisei, the old-timers. They told me their stories. Which, you could say, made me who I am today. "Shikata ga nai."

NEWMAN (*To the audience*): December 29, 1992. Marcus G. Dahlman's audition for *Face Value.*

MARCUS: Chinese folklore tells of the man who dreamt he was a butterfly. When morning came, the man awoke, and remembered he was not a butterfly, but a man. And that he knew, not a butterfly's joys and pains, but those of a man. He could only ask himself: am I really a man who dreamt he was a butterfly, or a butterfly now dreaming he's a man?

NEWMAN: Could you step outside for a moment, Marcus?

(Marcus exits the audition room.)

DHH: That was amazing!

NEWMAN: He's funny, vulnerable, strong.

DHH: I think he's a future star.

STUART: But guys, does he—? Does he look Asian to you?

DHH: What do you mean, "look Asian"?

STUART: Well, he doesn't seem to possess—any Asian features . . . at all.

DHH: And what exactly are "Asian features"?

STUART: He's got dark hair, but—

DHH: Short, high cheekbones, slanty eyes?

STUART: David—

DHH: I gotta say, I find your question sort of offensive. Asian faces come in a variety of shapes and sizes—just like any other human beings. Which we are, you know.

STUART: Miles, is he Asian?

NEWMAN: We managed to have a little conversation on the subject. He's not full-blooded—

DHH: He's Eurasian. You want to start discriminating against *them* now?

STUART: David, if our leading man, who's supposed to be an Asian dressing up in white face—if when he takes off his makeup, he still looks white—would that bother you?

DHH: "Looks white"—to whom? Other white people?

STUART: Just to put this on the table—you're certain you're not jumping at this actor because we're ten days away from the start of rehearsals and we don't have any other choices?

DHH: I'm excited because I think Marcus could be the next John Lone or BD Wong.

STUART: At least *they* both look Asian.

DHH: I have to cast this in a way that feels right to *me*. And I can tell an Asian when I see one.

THE ANNOUNCER: *Boston Globe*, January 1, 1993:

BOSTON GLOBE, JANUARY 1, 1993: Rehearsals have begun for David Henry Hwang's new play, *Face Value*, which will have its pre-Broadway tryout here, February 9–28 at the Colonial Theatre. The cast includes:

JANE: Jane Krakowski.

MARK: And Mark Linn-Baker. *(To the audience)* We all enjoyed working with Marcus immensely, he was a nice guy and very talented.

JANE: We did notice that he didn't look particularly Asian.

MARK: But it wasn't the kind of thing you come right out and ask someone.

JANE: And everyone else said he was Asian.

MARK: I did notice one other thing about Marcus, that he kind of kept to himself all through rehearsals.

JANE: But I remember—at the opening night party, out of town in Boston—it's like he was trying to tell me something.

MARCUS: You know, Jane, I—I haven't really had a chance to tell you this, but you're really great in the show.

JANE: Thanks. You, too!

MARCUS: Really?

JANE: Believe me, I've worked with some so-called stars who haven't got half as much talent as you do. And, of course, opportunities have been so limited for you.

MARCUS: What's that supposed to mean?

JANE: Well, before this, you've probably only gotten to play waiters and laundrymen and take-out delivery boys.

MARCUS: No, not really. Actually, I've played lots of parts.

JANE: In San Francisco, right?

MARCUS: Just last season, at San Jose Rep, in *The Glass Menagerie*, I played the Gentleman Caller.

JANE: And I'm sure you were amazing. Hey, you should see the kind of typecasting I have to deal with.

MARCUS: That's my point. I don't get typecast.

JANE: C'mon, Marcus, everybody gets typecast. What you mean, is that you don't get typecast as an Asian.

MARCUS: I guess you're right. Look, Jane, I like you a lot.

JANE: How much have you had to drink tonight?

MARCUS: Too much. I have to get something off my chest.

JANE: Well, don't say anything you'll regret in the morning.

MARCUS: Jane, I'm a fake.

JANE: Is that all?

MARCUS: Huh?

JANE: Welcome to the club. That comes with success. The higher you get, the more you feel you don't belong there. Like they put your name on the wrong list, and you somehow managed to sneak into the party.

MARCUS: That's exactly what happened!

JANE: You know how many other actors auditioned for your part?

MARCUS: Not enough? Jane, the show in Marin where they saw me—I was playing the white guy!

JANE: Just like you played the Gentleman Caller, right? *(Pause)* Marcus, you know what I do? When I'm feeling nervous around people, I just imagine I'm playing a part.

MARCUS: Yeah?

JANE: I picture who I want to be, then I start acting. Try it sometime, you'll be surprised.

MARCUS: Thanks, Jane—you've really been a big help to me.

JANE: Marcus, you are a fine fine actor. You just have to believe in yourself a little, that's all.

(Marcus exits the party.)

(To DHH) Marcus has had a lot to drink tonight.

DHH: Bet he never dreamed he'd end up in a Broadway show the day he got cast as a Japanese American soldier at the Marin Community Center.

JANE: We expecting reviews tomorrow morning?

DHH: Yeah. We still have work to do. But I think the critics will be encouraging.

JANE: Knock on wood. *(Pause)* Oh—and David, just so you know—that show in Marin? Marcus didn't play a Japanese American soldier.

DHH: He was in the play, I read an interview.

JANE: Oh, he was in it, all right. But he was the white guy.

THE ANNOUNCER: *Boston Globe*, February 15, 1993:

BOSTON GLOBE, FEBRUARY 15, 1993: Hwang's *Face Value* flops on its farce.

THE ANNOUNCER: *Christian Science Monitor:*

CHRISTIAN SCIENCE MONITOR: *Face Value* takes on more than it can deliver.

THE ANNOUNCER: *Boston Phoenix:*

BOSTON PHOENIX #1: *M. Turkey.*

THE ANNOUNCER: *New York Times:*

NEW YORK TIMES, FEBRUARY 26, 1993: The critical splat in Boston of David Henry Hwang's Broadway-bound *Face Value* ...

BOSTON GLOBE, FEBRUARY 15, 1993: Unsalvageable.

NEW YORK TIMES, FEBRUARY 26, 1993: —has the creative team now engaged in revamping a show that was essentially judged confusing and unfunny.

BOSTON PHOENIX #2: An embarrassment that should never have been allowed to happen.

THE ANNOUNCER: Michael Riedel, *TheaterWeek:*

MICHAEL RIEDEL: And where was playwright Hwang while Ostrow was rallying the troops? In his hotel room, rewriting furiously. Hwang, sounding upbeat for a man whose work has been called an embarrassment, said that he found being in trouble out of town—

DHH: exhilarating. —Of course, I would have loved to have gotten good reviews, but this is the situation we're in, so we're dealing with it.

(1980s-style disco music. A telephone rings.)

BOOKSTORE OWNER *(Into store phone)*: Sticky Fingers Books and Videos. Yeah, we got buttplugs. Come see for yourself, bye. *(Hangs up)*

(DHH approaches the Bookstore Owner.)

Hello. What've we got here? *Oriental Pearls, Enormous Lotus Blossoms, Banzai Babes.*

DHH: Do you take Visa?

BOOKSTORE OWNER: Sorry, just cash—say, aren't you David Henry Hwang?

DHH: Um . . .

BOOKSTORE OWNER: Yeah! You're David Henry Hwang, aren't you? Saw your picture in the Sunday paper.

DHH: You know, I never get recognized. Anywhere.

BOOKSTORE OWNER: You're doing a show, right? At the Colonial?

DHH: Um, yeah.

BOOKSTORE OWNER: *Face . . . Face*—

DHH: *Face Value.*

BOOKSTORE OWNER: Yeah, *Face Value.* Sounds really interesting. All that race and stuff.

DHH: We—didn't get such good reviews.

BOOKSTORE OWNER: Critics. What do they know, huh? You wrote that other one, right?

DHH: Yeah.

BOOKSTORE OWNER: That *Miss Saigon?*

DHH: No, that wasn't—

BOOKSTORE OWNER: You're a famous man.

DHH: Not usually.

BOOKSTORE OWNER: And I'm happy to see from your choice of material that you support your people.

DHH: Oh, those! Well I, er—yes, I try to—

BOOKSTORE OWNER: How 'bout I throw in a copy of *Asian Cravin'* on the house?

DHH: That's very kind, but—

BOOKSTORE OWNER: My pleasure. Gotta let someone do something nice for you once in a while—you know? Anthony Agoglia. Pleasure meeting you, Mr. Hwang.

DHH: David. Guess I'd better get . . . back to work now.

BOOKSTORE OWNER: You do that. *(Pause)* Oh—and David? Screw the critics, okay?

DHH: Thanks. *(To the audience)* I went back to my room and started rewriting. And yet—a little voice kept echoing in my head:

JANE: Oh, he was in it all right. But he was the white guy . . . the white guy . . . the white guy . . .

DHH: I decided to call Rodney Hatamiya, the actor who had worked with Marcus in *Go for Broke.*

(A phone rings.)

RODNEY: Hello?

DHH: Rodney! Hi, it's David Hwang.

RODNEY: Are you in New York?

DHH: No, Boston.

RODNEY: So—how's the show going?

DHH: Oh, well . . .

RODNEY: How's Marcus?

DHH: He's doing great. Listen, I wanted to ask—

RODNEY: He's one lucky motherfucker.

DHH: What do you mean?

RODNEY: That you're the one who cast him.

DHH: I don't quite—

RODNEY: Anyone else would have their balls handed back to them on a plate by our community. But fucking David Henry Hwang—*he* can cast a white guy as an Asian and no one gives a goddamn!

DHH: Marcus isn't Asian?

RODNEY: Say what?

DHH: I could tell he's not a hundred percent.

RODNEY: Marcus is a hundred percent, all right. One hundred percent white! You mean, you thought he was—?

DHH: Eurasian!

RODNEY: You got *that* half right. *(Pause)* Oh god, this is the funniest thing I've ever—can you imagine? If this got into the papers? "Leader of *Miss Saigon* protest casts white guy as Asian—by mistake!"

DHH: He's not.

RODNEY: Huh?

DHH: He's not. Marcus. He's not one hundred percent white.

RODNEY: C'mon!

DHH: His father is Jewish.

RODNEY: Last time I checked, Jewish was still white.

DHH: Not necessarily.

RODNEY: Not what?

DHH: Judaism is a religion, not a race.

RODNEY: It's sort of both, isn't it?

DHH: Like the way a wave and a particle are the same, yet different.

RODNEY: What?

DHH: Jews are both waves and particles.

RODNEY: What the fuck are you talking about?

DHH: Sammy Davis, Jr.! *He* was Jewish, wasn't he?

RODNEY: So Marcus's father is the Asian Sammy Davis, Jr.?

DHH: Maybe.

RODNEY: David—

DHH: I mean, I mean, do you even know where his Jewish ancestors came from?

RODNEY: Russia.

DHH: Oh.

RODNEY: I think he told me once—what city—

DHH: Siberia!

RODNEY: Huh?

DHH: Marcus's father—came from Siberia.

RODNEY: Are you sure? Because—

DHH: We talked about it! Extensively!

RODNEY: Even if you're right—how does that make him—?

DHH: Don't you know where Siberia is?

RODNEY: Near the North Pole?

DHH: Asia! Siberia is in Asia! Yes! And Marcus's father—is a Siberian Jew!

RODNEY: But Marcus doesn't look Asian!

DHH: Does Lou Diamond Phillips look Asian?

RODNEY: Well, sort of, if you—

DHH: Does Keanu Reeves?

RODNEY: Keanu Reeves is Asian?

DHH: Eurasian. Just like Marcus. Listen, Rodney, it's a new world out there. The demographics of this country are changing so fast—and sometimes we think it's only white people who gotta adjust. But *we've* gotta start thinking differently, too. "Free your mind / And the rest will follow / Be color-blind / Don't be so shallow!"

RODNEY: You're sure you're not making all this up to save your ass?

DHH: Rodney! Who stepped up to the line during the *Miss Saigon* fight?

RODNEY: Well, you—

DHH: Did I worry about saving my own ass *then*?

RODNEY: Sorry, I didn't mean to—

DHH: And another thing, Rodney. I loved your audition.

RODNEY: You did?

DHH: It was so honest. That's what I love most in the theater—honesty.

RODNEY: But I never got called back!

DHH: Lots of times, the best auditions are the ones you don't have to call back. You just know.

RODNEY: Then . . . why didn't you cast me?

DHH: Why?

RODNEY: I mean, I thought I did a fucking good job, too, but—

DHH: You're too good-looking.

RODNEY: Yeah?

DHH: I'm writing this character who's insecure, unsure of his masculinity—and who's going to believe that about you?

RODNEY: He's insecure because everyone thinks Asian men are nerds with little dicks.

DHH: Like I said, who's gonna believe that about you?

RODNEY: But, then—wouldn't it make your point even better to cast a guy like me?

DHH: That's just what I've been thinking.

RODNEY: You have?

DHH: I'm calling to check your availability. Once we get to New York—to bring you out, maybe first to understudy, but then eventually—to take over the part.

RODNEY: Shit, really? You're fucking offering me—?

DHH: Of course, the play would have to settle into a healthy run first.

RODNEY: Of course.

DHH: So. We just all have to do what we can—to make sure the show's a success. *(Pause)* Right?

RODNEY: Right.

CRAVER: But, David, you can't fire him.

THE ANNOUNCER: William Craver, David's agent.

DHH: What do you mean, I can't fire him?

CRAVER: For being white? That would be a violation of antidiscrimination laws.

DHH: How?

CRAVER: You'd be firing him because of his race.

DHH: But I hired him because of his race—or what I *thought* was his race!

CRAVER: Everyone just sort of lets that one slide.

DHH: So—I can hire on the basis of race, but not fire for that same reason?

CRAVER: Right.

DHH: Why?

CRAVER: Because people don't generally sue someone for hiring them!

DHH: So I'm stuck with this guy forever, no matter what?

CRAVER: Of course you can fire him. For any reason other than his race.

DHH: Marcus and I have really gotta talk.

CRAVER: No! Whatever you do, he can't know that you know he's white. Once that happens, then you really *can't* ever fire him.

DHH: Shit! We're speaking to a group of Asian American students tonight. They'll see right through him. Then they'll blow the whistle, then I won't be able to fire him, then—

CRAVER: David, David—why don't you just do all the talking at this event?

DHH: Okay, okay—I can do this. I can get through this thing tonight. Then, tomorrow, we can get rid of him.

CRAVER: He'll be out of your life forever.

DHH: Great. So long as I help Marcus pass as an Asian, I can still fire him for being white.

CRAVER: Right.

GISH JEN: Welcome to the Asian American Resource Center. I'm Gish Jen.

DHH: Marcus, I've been doing a little thinking—

MARCUS: Yeah?

GISH JEN: I'm so pleased to see you all at tonight's event.

DHH: About your name.

GISH JEN: An evening with the creators of *Face Value*.

DHH: Marcus G. Dahlman. Have you ever thought about taking a stage name?

MARCUS: Like what?

DHH: How 'bout just, "Marcus Gee"?

GISH JEN: So without any further delay—

MARCUS: I never—

GISH JEN: Please welcome David Henry Hwang and Marcus—

DHH *(At Gish)*: Marcus Gee!

(Applause.)

STUDENT #1: Your play? Man, you guys have made a beautiful thing.

DHH: Thank you, that's very—

STUDENT #1: And when I read those reviews, I thought, Shit, they're doing it to us again.

STUDENT #2: Tell 'em, brother!

STUDENT #1: They can't stand it when a yellow man gets too much power in their world.

STUDENT #2: You got that right!

STUDENT #1: So they got no choice—but to take us down! You and Spike Lee, man!

MARCUS: Thank you. When did you see our show?

STUDENT #1: I don't have to see it to know what's going on here.

DHH: You could tell, just by reading the reviews.

STUDENT #1: That's right! Once those white critics started beating on your show, I knew it must be great.

DHH: You can really see through the hype. *(To Student #3)* Yes?

STUDENT #3: I saw your show a couple of nights ago.

DHH: Yes?

MARCUS: Yes?

STUDENT #3: It was amazing.

DHH: Thank you.

MARCUS: Thank you.

STUDENT #3: But I do have one question for Marcus. What *are* you, anyway?

DHH: You mean, what is he *really*?

(Laughter.)

MARCUS: Well, my ancestry's really mixed-up, but there are some who say that the Lost Tribe of Israel—

DHH: Marcus is Eurasian. That's the bottom line, isn't it, Marcus?

MARCUS: Well, yes, I suppose—

DHH: Yes?

STUDENT #4: Marcus, your ancestors—I mean, the Asian part, where did they come from?

DHH: Siberia, didn't they? *(Pause)* We spoke about that once. *(Pause)* They were Russian Siberian Asian Jews? Weren't they?

MARCUS: Yeah, sure . . .

STUDENT #4: Siberian. Wow. I've never really heard of—

DHH: Oh, they're a rapidly growing minority. In the next few years, you're going to see an explosion of Siberian American culture in this country—Siberian restaurants, folk festivals, artists, and the emergence of Little Siberia towns all over America.

STUDENT #4: And Siberians—are Asians?

DHH: Here, I just happen to be carrying an atlas. See, it's just north of China. Perhaps the most well-known Siberian right now—besides Marcus, of course—is a model named Irina Pantaeva. Oh, look, here she is—in the most recent issue of *Cosmopolitan. (He flashes a picture of a Siberian model with very Asian features)* Nowadays, we really don't "all look alike." Looks don't matter any longer. Marcus is like us— he's an American.

STUDENT #3: Marcus, as an actor of Jewish Siberian heritage— have you faced a lot of barriers?

DHH *(To Marcus)*: Sure you have. You can tell them.

MARCUS: Well, uh, before this, my career was sort of going nowhere. I mean, directors just didn't seem to know what to do with me.

STUDENT #1: Bastards!

MARCUS: Last November, I went in on this commercial call. They had me back five times. Five times! And in the end, you know what they told me? They said I didn't "look right."

(Gasps all around.)

STUDENT #2: That is so racist!

STUDENT #4: Marcus, did you celebrate Siberian traditions at home?

MARCUS: No, not really. Though we did have this little music box on the mantel that played "Somewhere My Love," and—

DHH: Next?

STUDENT #3: Was growing up hard for you?

DHH *(To Marcus)*: Yeah, it was, right?

MARCUS: Well, yeah—see, when I was seven, my parents moved to this fancy neighborhood because it had good schools. But that made me sort of . . . the poor kid in town.

STUDENT #2: I know what that's like.

YELLOW FACE

MARCUS: You do? Um, thank you.

STUDENT #1: Bastards!

MARCUS: You really wanna hear this?

DHH: Trust me, they do.

MARCUS: See the other kids all knew the truth about me. So on the outside, I was trying to fit in with everyone else, but inside, um . . .

STUDENT #2: You knew they were lookin' down on you!

MARCUS: That's right! God, this is so weird, I've never even . . . and in public like this . . .

STUDENT #2: Marcus, we've all been oppressed!

STUDENT #1: By the bastards! Now you say it!

MARCUS: Huh? Me? No, I—

STUDENT #1: No, man, ya gotta say it!

STUDENT #2: It's the only way you're gonna rise up!

MARCUS: See it was subtle—I mean, it wasn't like—

STUDENT #2: Subtle sucks.

STUDENT #1: C'mon, ya gotta say it!

MARCUS: Okay. Bastards.

STUDENT #1: That's right. Those motherfuckers. Who make us feel like shit—they were—

MARCUS: Bastards! You're right, they were mean little bastards!

(Everyone applauds.)

STUDENT #2: Doesn't that feel good, Marcus?

MARCUS: It really does! God, this is amazing, you guys don't even know me—and to welcome me like this into your club—

DHH: Community.

MARCUS: Community. I feel like I've finally found—a home—

STUDENT #2: We love you, brother!

MARCUS: Do you know how special this is? Out there—in the rest of America—everyone's on their own, fighting to stay afloat. But *you*—you've got each other. No, *we've* got each other!

STUDENT #4: Marcus Gee, you are a role model for us all!

MARCUS: I wouldn't even be here today—if I hadn't had the good fortune to be cast in a play by David Henry Hwang! *(Applause peaks)*

(A phone rings.)

DHH: Stuart? Sorry to call so late at night. But do you think BD's still available? *(Pause)* I don't think Marcus is working out.

(A phone rings, followed by the "beep" of an answering machine.)

MARCUS: David, it's Marcus. Er, could we talk? It's 10:30 in the morning, and I just got a call from the producers. This is kind of important. Call me. Please.

(Another "beep.")

It's eleven o'clock. Look, it's really important . . . that you and I talk. Okay?

(Another "beep.")

I'm assuming you know what's going on, and—if this is what you want, I understand. I'd just like the chance to hear it from you.

(Another "beep.")

It's Marcus. I'm at Logan Airport. My flight starts boarding in twenty minutes.

(Another "beep.")

It's final call. I'm heading back to San Francisco. Look, I just wanted to thank you. I've gotten to work with some wonderful artists and—and maybe even, through everything that happened—understand a little better who I am. Talk to you sometime, okay?

(Recording: "To delete your messages, press 7." DHH presses a key. Recording: "Messages deleted.")

THE ANNOUNCER: Associated Press, March 15, 1993:
ASSOCIATED PRESS, MARCH 15, 1993: *Face Value*, the new Broadway comedy by the author of *M. Butterfly*, closed

before its official opening, shutting down after eight preview performances at a loss of more than two million dollars.

(A phone rings.)

MARGARET FUNG: Hello?

DHH: Margaret?

MARGARET FUNG: David?

THE ANNOUNCER: Margaret Fung, executive director, Asian American Legal Defense and Education Fund.

DHH: Yeah, it's David Hwang. David *Henry* Hwang.

MARGARET FUNG: Are you drunk?

DHH: No. No! Well, maybe just a little. Listen, I don't know if you heard about my show—it kinda . . . closed.

MARGARET FUNG: Yes, you told me last night.

DHH: Do you think I'm still an Asian American role model?

MARGARET FUNG: David, it's two a.m.!

DHH: But, Margaret!—

MARGARET FUNG: Yes, David, you're still a role model. Now—

DHH: You know, that Legal Defense thing, the one you run?—

MARGARET FUNG: AALDEF.

DHH: Yeah, that. Do you think you could give me one of your Justice in Action Awards?

MARGARET FUNG: David, you've already received one.

DHH: But I mean, could I get another one?

MARGARET FUNG: Well, we like to think of it as kind of a life-time achievement award. Which means we only give out one per lifetime.

DHH: My show—I was the victim of racism, right?

MARGARET FUNG: Don't you have anyone else you can call? I mean, we hardly know each other!

DHH: Yeah, but I've always thought—when it comes to civil rights attorneys?—that you are . . . kinda hot.

MARGARET FUNG: I'm going to hang up now.

DHH: But, Margaret!—

MARGARET FUNG: Yes, David, you were the victim of racism. Now, good night.

(Dong Track #15: "Cicadas Are Crying, I Sigh as My Youth Passes By.")

MARCUS: Dear David, I'm still here in the Dong village—it's been three weeks. I thought I would have moved on by now—maybe to some of the other minority communities, spread out over China—did you know there are more than fifty groups in all? But I think what's kept me here in Dong country—is the music. *(Pause)* I've done some research. Turns out, the "big song" came to China over the Silk Road, a thousand years ago. Now I sit, in the center of the village at twilight, and listen, with my eyes shut. And sometimes, when I'm very lucky, I can hear the whole journey—from the Carpathian Mountains, through the Middle East, all the way into Asia, covering half the world. The Dong learn this music from birth—it's so much a part of who they are—of who I'm not. And yet all these songs once came from somewhere else—sorta like me.

(A phone rings. Music out.)

DHH: Hello?
HYH: Hello? Son?
DHH: Hi, Dad.
HYH: I was just calling to see how you're doing.
DHH: Me? I'm great. Things are great.
HYH: And how are things—money-wise?
DHH: Dad—
HYH: I thought you'd want to know—I just made a big donation—to your friend, Bill Clinton.
DHH: He's not my friend, I just—
HYH: You supported him, didn't you? I talked to this guy from his campaign—told him I want to start a new group: "Chinese Republican Bankers for Clinton."
DHH: Would there be any other members?
HYH: Lots! Did you hear that Pat Buchanan? Wants to kick us all out of the country! The Clinton guy—he loved my idea.
DHH: That's great, Dad. Listen, I'm—
HYH: Now, I can finally become Ambassador to Great Britain.
DHH: What?
HYH: Or China. I would settle for China.
DHH: But you're not a diplomat!

HYH: I'm a businessman, aren't I? Dave, this is how things work. You scratch my back, I'll scratch yours. Win-win! It's the American way.

DHH: You know you're one of the least diplomatic people in the world.

HYH: I know, isn't it beautiful? I'll do it just like Frank: "My Way."

DHH: Dad, I can't really think about this right now—

HYH: I know. Son, why don't you come on the board of my bank?

DHH: What?

HYH: Marty DeLuca just died, there's an empty space to fill.

DHH: But I don't know the first thing about banking.

HYH: You used to work in the bank! Back in college, during the summers, remember?

DHH: As a teller!

HYH: And you were a good teller too. Every night, your drawer balanced.

DHH: And what's my title going to be? "Director of Nepotism"?

HYH: If that's the title you want, fine, you can have it.

DHH: Dad, I'm not in the least qualified.

HYH: What do you mean, you're not qualified? You're my son, aren't you? *(Pause)* You know, we pay our board members honorarium for attending meetings. Just a few thousand dollars, but better than nothing. You'll come out to L.A. every month—you can stay at our house—your mother will be so happy to cook for you.

DHH: Dad?

HYH: And maybe you'll even decide you like banking.

DHH: Just out of curiosity—

HYH: Huh?

DHH: Is that a few thousand dollars a year, or per meeting?

BEATRICE CHANG: And total assets as of October 31 stand at $532,400,000.

THE ANNOUNCER: Far East National Bank board meeting. Present are:

DON MIHAIL: Don Mihail, vice-chair.

BEATRICE CHANG: Beatrice Chang, chief financial officer.

HYH: Henry Hwang, chairman of the board. Just like Frank. *(To the others)* I need a motion to approve the budget.

DON MIHAIL *(Eastern European accent)*: So moved.

HYH: Second? *(Pause)* Second?
DHH: Oh! Second.
HYH: That's good, Son.
DON MIHAIL: He's learning fast.
HYH: All in favor, say "aye."
DON MIHAIL, DHH AND HYH: Aye!
HYH: All opposed? *(Pause)* Okay, we found office space—right in the center of Beijing. Brand-new building, beautiful.
DON MIHAIL: Henry, congratulations! This is a big deal.
HYH: Don, I'm so excited! The system over there—they need our help.
DON MIHAIL: And lots of business there too!
HYH: It's win-win! I'm telling you, I feel like a pioneer, like a Yankee trader. Beatrice?
BEATRICE CHANG: On Monday, we are putting out a press release to announce the opening of our Beijing office. Far East will become the first American bank to do business in the People's Republic of China.
HYH: In Beijing—after I signed the lease—our new landlords took me to a karaoke bar. And guess what I sang? You'll never guess.
DHH: "My Way."
HYH: That's right! They were so moved. It was beautiful. — Meeting adjourned.
DON MIHAIL: David, the wife and I went out last night—to a musical show.
DHH: Yeah? What'd you see?
DON MIHAIL: *The King and I.* And, David—that guy who played the King—you know him!
DHH: I know a lot of Asian actors. What was his name?
DON MIHAIL: What was his name? He was in one of your plays.
DHH: Which one?
DON MIHAIL: *Face the Facts*, or—
DHH: *Face Value?*
DON MIHAIL: Yes, yes!
DHH: BD Wong is in *The King and I?*
DON MIHAIL: No, no—that wasn't his name.
DHH: But who else could it—no!
DON MIHAIL: He had a Chinese name.
DHH: It can't be.

DON MIHAIL: Strange thing, though—he didn't look very Chinese.

("Shall We Dance?" plays. The ensemble becomes actors taking a curtain call from The King and I. *Marcus, as the King, enters to take the final bow. DHH watches, aghast. Lights fade.)*

Act Two

The lights come up on DHH, obsessively reading newspaper clippings. "Shall We Dance" plays.

THE ANNOUNCER: *Los Angeles Times:*
LOS ANGELES TIMES: The most significant thing about this *King and I* is its ethnic-authentic casting—
DHH *(Reading)*: —and convincing South Asian look? Aw, Jesus!
THE ANNOUNCER: *Boston Globe:*
DHH: Mr. Gee's warm humanity fills this exquisite *King and I.*
THE ANNOUNCER: *Seattle Times:*
DHH: Gee throws off the ghost of Yul Brenner and reinvents the King for our multicultural age.

(Music out.)

HYH: Montreal, Boston, Houston, Seattle— Son, are these clippings all about you?
DHH: Not really, Dad, see, I—
HYH: Hey, it's that guy—Marcus Gee! You gave him his start, Son.
DHH: Don't remind me.
HYH *(Reading to himself)*: Mmmm. Hmmmm. Mmmm. Hmmmm.
DHH: What now?!

HYH: He's very deep. Listen to this:

MARCUS: "Never let anyone tell you that what you look like is who you are. Those are the limitations we have to fight. Even people who look like me. Especially people who look like me."

HYH: Beautiful!

DHH: I am going to throw up.

HYH: You know, Dave, *you* should say stuff like that.

DHH: *I* should—? Where do you think he got it? I said those very words! When he was in my show!

HYH: Then you teach him well, you must be so proud!

DHH: Dad, he's a disaster. I thought I got rid of him back in Boston, but no, he keeps popping up—as if from the grave— just to torture me.

HYH: You think you getting a little worked up about this?

DHH: Dad, his name isn't "Gee"! He's not even Asian!

(Pause.)

HYH: You know, I had that thought. When I first saw him in your show, I thought, He's not Chinese. But now that I read his words, who cares? Maybe, in my heart, if I can be Gary Cooper or Clark Gable, then maybe—in his?—he can be Marcus Gee.

DHH: I didn't go through all those protests and hunger strikes just so some white imposter could help himself to our hard-won opportunities.

HYH: You went on a hunger strike?

DHH: Sure, back in college with the other Asian students. For two whole weeks!

HYH: You didn't eat for two weeks? You could've been—!

DHH: Dad, I'm not stupid, of course I ate.

HYH: But you said—

DHH: We fasted in shifts.

THE ANNOUNCER: *Variety*, April 27, 1996:

VARIETY: Asian kudos announced. The newly formed Asian American Artists Association announced honorees for their first annual Warrior Awards. Legit scribe David Henry Hwang (*M. Butterfly*) will receive a "Visionary Warrior Award" from the org, which was founded by Asian American film exec—

FRITZ: Fritz Friedman. David, sweetheart, follow me. By the way, your hair looks terrific. *(Pause)* We've arranged a little impromptu press conference with the community media. You don't mind answering questions, do you?

DHH: Of course not.

FRITZ: Just stand here. Journalists, please welcome David Henry Hwang.

(Light applause, cameras click.)

DHH: I'm so pleased to be honored by the Asian American Artists Association, or AAAA— *(Pronounced "Aaaaah")*

FRITZ: Oh! Here comes another of tonight's awardees. Our "Most Promising Newcomer Warrior": Marcus Gee— *(Bigger applause, more cameras click)* —who's managed to join us tonight, despite his grueling tour schedule in *The King and I*. *(To Marcus and DHH)* You two know each other? Well, who doesn't know Marcus, right?

MARCUS: Know each other? David gave me my first job! How ya doin', bro? We haven't talked since, when . . . ?

DHH: Since I, uh, since you were in—

MARCUS: *Face Value*. Thanks for the break, buddy!

(Marcus gives DHH a 1990s-style "soul" handshake. Cameras click.)

REPORTERS: Marcus! Marcus!

REPORTER #1: Marcus, your performance in *The King and I* has been getting rave reviews all around the country. Did you have any reservations about taking a role that some in the community have labeled stereotypical?

MARCUS: Of course I did. I feel like one of the most important responsibilities for any actor of color is to be true to his or her community, to make sure we only put out positive images. I only agreed to be seen for the role of the King after the producers assured me that the hallmark of this production would be cultural authenticity.

(Later. DHH and Marcus.)

Hey, bro!

DHH: Don't give me that, "Hey bro" shit.

MARCUS: Sorry, I didn't mean to offend.

DHH: Well, you are. I mean, this whole thing you're doing, it's really offensive.

MARCUS: Is this all about what happened in Boston?

DHH: Of course it's about what happened in Boston!

MARCUS: Dave, for me, it turned out to be a blessing in disguise!

DHH: You're really going to act like you don't know?

MARCUS: I wish I could say I was acting. But I'm not that good an actor. At least, *you* didn't think so.

DHH: You're running around. Pretending to be Asian. You're lying! To everyone! There—can you follow that?

(Pause.)

MARCUS: I am trying really hard not to lie. Okay, now and then, I have to mention the Siberian thing, and that's unfortunate, but, as much as possible—I am doing my best to speak only the truth.

DHH: Your whole life is a lie! You're letting people believe—

MARCUS: You said yourself, didn't you? It doesn't matter what someone looks like on the outside.

DHH: I didn't mean that literally!

MARCUS: Then how did you mean it? David, do you have a problem with anything I'm saying?

DHH: No, it's not *what* you're saying—

MARCUS: It's that *I'm* the one who's saying it? Doesn't that make your position kind of racist?

DHH: This is not that hard! In order to be Asian, you have to have at least some Asian blood!

MARCUS: I'm just saying some things that need to be said. Doing things that need to be done. I mean, *someone's* gotta step up.

DHH: What's that supposed to mean?

MARCUS: To be perfectly honest, I've been attending a lot of community functions lately. And I don't see you at any of them.

DHH: You can't be—

MARCUS: John Huang has founded this great new organization, the Asian Leadership Council.

DHH: You're lecturing *me*? On how to be Asian?

MARCUS: It's a chance for APAs to gain some real clout—by leveraging our donations to the presidential campaign.

DHH: I can't believe this!

MARCUS: They're honoring me next week in D.C. We could really use your support.

DHH: I was an Asian American role model back when you were still a Caucasian!

MARCUS: David, c'mon—is this a popularity contest?

DHH: No, I am not in a popularity contest with you.

MARCUS: This is about collective empowerment, agreed?

DHH: Fuck. That's so easy for you to say.

MARCUS: What?

DHH: You come in here with that, that face of yours. Call yourself Asian. Everyone falls at your feet. But you don't have to live as an Asian—every day of your life. No, you can just skim the cream, you, you, you ethnic tourist!

MARCUS: You're right. I don't *have* to live Asian every day of my life. I am *choosing* to do so.

DHH: Funny thing about race. You don't get to choose. If you'd been born a minority, you'd know that.

MARCUS: David, are you familiar with the Chinese concept of "face"?

DHH: Am *I*—? Of course—It's, it's, you know . . .

MARCUS: Basically, it says that the face we choose to show the world—reveals who we really are.

DHH: I knew that.

MARCUS: Well, I've chosen *my* face. And now I'm becoming the person I've always wanted to be.

LEAH *(Offstage)*: Marcus? *(Entering)* There you are, what's keeping you?

MARCUS: Sorry, hon. Just got talking with David.

LEAH *(To DHH)*: Oh, hi.

DHH: Hey, Leah—I hadn't seen you here.

LEAH: Surprise, surprise. *(To Marcus)* Better get onstage quick. They're about to auction off dinner with you. *(Gives Marcus a kiss)*

MARCUS: Oh, thanks. *(To DHH)* D.C., next week. Remember this name: John Huang. It's gonna be big.

(Marcus exits. Leah starts to follow.)

DHH: You're dating *him*?

LEAH: Yes. So?

DHH: Does he know that we—you and I—that we . . . ?

LEAH: Well, maybe, I might've mentioned—you know, it's not the first thing on my mind day and night.

DHH: Leah, you can't.

LEAH: Excuse me?

DHH: You can't . . . become his girlfriend.

LEAH: Well, funny thing, cuz I already am.

DHH: When did you meet him?

LEAH: It's none of your—

DHH: Was it before or after he got this job in *The King and I*?

LEAH: If you must know, we're touring together. I'm playing Tuptim. Again, don't ask. Now if you'll excuse me—

DHH: So he hasn't told you.

LEAH: Told me what?

DHH: You think he's Asian, don't you?

LEAH: Not a hundred percent, but—

DHH: I can't believe he's dating *you*. Of all people!

LEAH: Wait. You think he's dating *me*—to get back at *you*?

DHH: No, not just to get back at me. It's, it's, it's even weirder than that.

LEAH: Oh my god.

DHH: More diabolical.

LEAH: David, listen—

DHH: It's like, like he, he wants to *become* me.

LEAH: Whoa.

DHH: I know this sounds crazy, I can hardly believe it myself. But—but—

LEAH: Hey, hey! Earth to narcissist!

DHH: What's that supposed to mean?

LEAH: Yes, I *did* tell Marcus that you and I had been a couple. I mean, how could we have avoided the subject, you fired him, remember? But, David, whatever hurt and bitterness he may have felt towards you back then, it's gone now, okay? And, let's face it, even if he *had* done your play on Broadway, he'd only have ended up working for, like, one week longer.

DHH: Your *King and I* is gonna end one day, too, you know.

LEAH: So? I'm dating Marcus, not the King of Siam.

DHH: Leah, he's not Asian!

LEAH: David, no one's Asian enough for you.

DHH: That's not what I—

LEAH: Like, the way you used to criticize me for listening to The Cure.

DHH: I never—

LEAH: You thought my taste in music was too white!

DHH: I never said anything like—

LEAH: Yes, you did. You said, "Personally, I believe in supporting black artists."

DHH: I only meant, that as people of color, African American singers are more likely to share our struggles and understand our pain.

LEAH: Mariah Carey? C'mon, get real.

DHH: Leah, Marcus is not Asian. Literally. He's lying to you. And everyone around him. He's got this entire community fooled. The truth is, Marcus Gee is one hundred percent white.

(Pause.)

LEAH: David, are you still in touch with Dr. Wasserman?

DHH: You don't believe me.

LEAH: I believe you're in a really unhealthy place right now. And I think—I'm gonna go. *(Pause)* You should get back to writing plays.

(Dong Track #20: "I Am a Butterfly Searching for Flowers.")

MARCUS: Dear David, I've been here in Dong country three months now. And I've made a friend. Yen, this kid—I think he's probably like a Dong rebel. He refuses to sing the old songs, spends most of the year in Guiyang, working in the factories. And he speaks a little English. Yen told me the Dong rush out to sing for the tourists because they're paid by the provincial government. I guess he was trying to burst my bubble. *(Pause)* I have to admit, I was disappointed. Suddenly, all I could see were the satellite dishes all over the village. Then I noticed this farmer standing knee-deep in the river, catching fish with his bare hands—and a cell phone strapped to his belt. I thought, one slip and that phone's finished. Then suddenly, I realized, the guy's been doing this his whole life. He knows he's not gonna fall. Ever. So even if he does wear a cell phone, isn't he still amazing?

(A phone rings.)

JULIA DAHLMAN: Hello?

DHH: Hi, may I speak to Julia Dahlman?

JULIA DAHLMAN: That's me, honey, who's this?

DHH: My name is David Henry Hwang. I'm a playwright, and—

JULIA DAHLMAN: Why, of course, I know who you are. My son was in your play!

DHH: That's sort of why I'm calling. Are you aware that Marcus is going around claiming to be Asian?

JULIA DAHLMAN: Huh? Oh no, darling, he's *playing* an Asian. In *The King and I.*

DHH: Not just onstage. In interviews, he's telling people he actually has Asian blood. As his mother, doesn't that bother you?

JULIA DAHLMAN: Should it?

DHH: Don't you think you should tell him to stop?

JULIA DAHLMAN: What are you talking about?

DHH: I'm talking about truth. About honesty. Didn't you ever try to teach Marcus any of these—?

JULIA DAHLMAN: Stop. Just back up your truck, Mr. David. Don't you know anything at all about show business? Marcus is doing *The King and I.* Who do you think reporters want to talk to? The "King" or the "I." They ask him questions and what's he supposed to say? Nothing?

DHH: He's supposed to tell them that he's white!

JULIA DAHLMAN: David, this is America—where race shouldn't matter. I didn't even know about the racism Asians still face today. But Marcus raised my consciousness. He told me it doesn't matter what someone looks like on the outside. That is why he's giving his time and money to your good causes. And, frankly, you should be fucking grateful.

(DHH and Leah.)

LEAH: David, I really appreciate you meeting me like this.

DHH: Well, Leah, you asked in such a civil tone, it really threw me for a loop.

LEAH: I didn't want to talk about this over the phone, but—

DHH: What's wrong? Trouble in paradise? Catch your boyfriend putting butter on his rice?

LEAH: This is serious! Marcus is under investigation—by the government. It all started late one night—they called our home—

DHH: Wait. You and Marcus—are living together?

LEAH: Well, yeah, it just made sense—

DHH: And what were you two doing? Late at night?

LEAH: Nothing! Reading the paper, watching TV, I dunno.

DHH: Yeah, right.

(Leah and Marcus are making out. A phone rings.)

MARCUS: I should get that.

LEAH: You have got to be kidding. Let the machine pick up!

MARCUS: It might be something important.

LEAH: Whatever it is can wait. I can't.

(Marcus picks up the phone.)

MARCUS: Hello?

LEAH: Oh, you are in *such* trouble.

Rocco: Is this Marcus Gee?

MARCUS: Speaking.

ROCCO: I'm calling from the office of Senator Fred Thompson on behalf of the Committee on Governmental Affairs.

MARCUS: Do you realize that it's 11:30 at night?

ROCCO: Yes, I'm sorry. Would you mind answering some questions?

MARCUS: Can you call back in the morning?

ROCCO: The committee would be most grateful for your cooperation at this time. Our records show that you made a donation of $250. To the Asian Pacific American Leadership Council.

MARCUS: Yes, at their fundraising dinner in Washington last year.

ROCCO: Are you aware that their founder, John Huang, is under investigation? That a good number of the donations he gathered may have violated federal campaign laws?

MARCUS: What do you want from me?

ROCCO: Are you an American citizen?

MARCUS: What?!

ROCCO: Where are you from?

MARCUS: You mean, where am I *really* from?

(Pause.)

ROCCO: What do you mean by that?

MARCUS: I mean—never mind, it was a joke.

ROCCO: Why was that a joke?

MARCUS: Because Asians are always being asked, "Where are you really from?"

ROCCO: Who else has asked you this?

MARCUS: You're completely clueless, aren't you?

ROCCO: Why don't you clue me in? What is your ancestry?

MARCUS: My god, they can't even ask that at auditions!

ROCCO: Auditions?

MARCUS: I don't have to answer that question.

ROCCO: I suggest you do. Because there's something strange about your file. It seems you made your donation under a false name.

MARCUS: Well, yes, I—

ROCCO: You realize this is a violation of federal campaign laws?

MARCUS: I used my stage name. I didn't know that was illegal.

ROCCO: Why did you change your name?

MARCUS: To more—accurately reflect the roles I was playing.

ROCCO: And what sort of roles were those?

MARCUS: Asian roles.

ROCCO: So is it fair to assume that your ethnicity is actually Asian?

MARCUS: I don't have to answer that question.

ROCCO: We keep getting stuck on that one, don't we?

MARCUS: I'm going to hang up now.

ROCCO: That would be a bad idea.

MARCUS: This whole conversation is a bad idea. You guys are so on the wrong track. In fact, you know something?—you're idiots. *(Hangs up)*

(Dial tone.)

LEAH *(To DHH)*: We thought that would be the end of it, but now we're getting more calls—from the FBI, the Democratic National Committee.

DHH: So wait. Lemme get this straight: the government's investigating people who made donations to presidential campaigns—

LEAH: Asians. Just Asians. Cuz they think foreigners tried to influence the elections—anyone named "Lee" or "Wong" or—

DHH: And somehow Marcus got on their list?

LEAH: Can you believe it? He made a donation, using his stage name. There's gonna be a press conference tomorrow to expose this crap and— *(Pause)* David? *(Pause)* Why are you . . . laughing?

DHH: Well, he wanted to be Asian, didn't he? "Every day of my life!" Be careful what you wish for, kimosabe!

LEAH: I was hoping you'd show up at the press conference to help—

DHH: Moi? Marcus doesn't need *my* help. He's Captain Asian America! A role model for us all!

LEAH: David, listen—Asians? Accused of being evil foreigners? This is exactly the kind of shit they always throw at us.

DHH: Well, now they're throwing it at him. And it is making my day.

LEAH: I can't believe this. You used to stand for something. Now, it's, it's like you've turned into some kind of fake Asian.

DHH: Me? *I'm* the fake Asian? Someone's not looking in her own bed.

LEAH: Fuck you.

DHH: For your information, the reason I can't make your little press conference is cuz I'm doing something much more important for Asian Americans. You ever hear of network television? I'm working with this comedienne. On a brand-new series. She's Korean American—just like you. *(Pause)* Leah?

THE ANNOUNCER: On the set of *All-American Girl*, starring Miss Margaret Cho!

DHH: Margaret, hi! I've been hired to take the show in a new direction: more Asian. So—use chopsticks. Use chopsticks! And when you're done you can put them in your hair. *(Pause)* And Margaret—you're wearing shoes, which is something we don't do in the house. Take off your shoes. We don't wear shoes in the house. *(Pause)* Now, I am going to leave this abacus right here . . .

THE ANNOUNCER: *New York Times*, September 12, 1997:

NEW YORK TIMES, SEPTEMBER 12, 1997: Today, eighteen Asian American groups filed a complaint with the United States Commission on Civil Rights.

MARCUS: I was harassed by midnight telephone calls, my integrity was slandered, and my citizenship was questioned.

NEW YORK TIMES, SEPTEMBER 12, 1997: Leaders of Asian American groups say this telephone call and twelve hundred others to Asian American contributors are part of a harassment of people of Asian descent.

THE ANNOUNCER: *USA Today*, July 9, 1997:

USA TODAY: [Congress] yesterday began long-awaited hearings on the campaign finance improprieties of 1996 with ... an assertion [by committee chair Fred Thompson, Republican of Tennessee]—

FRED THOMPSON: High-level Chinese government officials crafted a plan to increase China's influence over the U.S. political process. Our investigation suggests the plan continues today.

THE ANNOUNCER: Senator Bob Bennett, Republican of Utah:

SENATOR BENNETT: In my opinion, [these] activities are classic activities on the part of an Asian who comes out of that culture.

THE ANNOUNCER: Senator Sam Brownback, Republican of Kansas:

SENATOR BROWNBACK: Two Huangs don't make a right.

THE ANNOUNCER: Senator Richard Shelby, Republican of Alabama:

SENATOR SHELBY: We've got to remember the Chinese are everywhere ... They're real. They're here. And probably ... very crafty people.

THE ANNOUNCER: Representative Tom DeLay, Republican of Texas:

REPRESENTATIVE DELAY: There's a high probability this is money from foreign[ers] ... if you're friends with a guy named Johnny Huang [or Marcus Gee] ... and you have friend[s] by the name of Arief and Soraya, and I cannot even pronounce [these] name[s] ... Cheong Am, Yogesh Gandhi, Lap Seng Ng— *(Tries different pronunciations)* Ng? . . . Ng?

THE ANNOUNCER: Representative Jack Kingston, Republican of Georgia:

REPRESENTATIVE KINGSTON: Illegal campaign contributions are just the tip of the egg roll.

THE ANNOUNCER: Senator Brownback:

SENATOR BROWNBACK: John Huang brought in so much money for the Democrats, because under his salary agreement, no raise money, no get bonus.

THE ANNOUNCER: *New York Times,* March 6, 1999: China stole nuclear secrets from Los Alamos. Written by—

(Sound cue: "Name Withheld on Advice of Counsel.")

NAME WITHHELD ON ADVICE OF COUNSEL (NWOAOC): Government officials [have] administered lie-detector tests to . . . a Los Alamos computer scientist who is Chinese American . . . This is going to be just as bad as the Rosenbergs, [an official] recalled saying.

(The sound of paper coming out of an old thermal-style fax machine. HYH crosses to DHH, carrying fax paper.)

HYH: Dave! Dave, look! A fax—for you!

DHH: So? Why are you getting all—?

HYH: From Marcus Gee!

DHH: God, get that away from me. He probably wants money or something.

MARCUS *(Reading)*: Dear David—

DHH: I don't want to hear it!

HYH: Sssh! I'm reading for myself!

MARCUS: Did you see that story in the *New York Times?* About Wen Ho Lee, the Chinese American nuclear scientist they're accusing of treason?

HYH: Marcus says they're holding a rally to stand up for Wen Ho Lee. And they want you to join them. *(Pause)* Well? Are you gonna go?

DHH: Of course I'm not gonna go!

HYH: But—

DHH: Do you see what I'm doing here? I'm preparing a pitch for a movie project.

HYH: But Marcus says—

DHH: Aw, Jesus!

MARCUS: I'm sorry you couldn't make our press conference exposing the phone calls but—it's all snowballing: first, the campaign finance scandals, and now, Wen Ho Lee. This country is gearing up to make China its next big enemy. And, as usual, who do they go after first? Asian Americans.

DHH: That guy is so paranoid. Hey, maybe Wen Ho Lee's actually guilty. Ever think of that? And if he's not, what's Marcus so worried about? Doesn't he know we have rights in this country? *(To the audience)* Only in my research for this play, did I finally read a transcript of Wen Ho Lee's interrogation by the FBI, March 7, 1999:

FBI AGENT: Washington is under the impression that you're a spy. And this [*New York Times*] article is doing everything but coming out with your name ... Everything is pointing to you ...

WEN HO LEE: I'm just telling you, I believe truth, and I believe honest, and I know, I know myself, I did not tell anything ... okay? I told you more than ten times ... eventually something will be clear-cut, okay?

FBI AGENT: What are you going to tell your friends? What are you going to tell your family? What are you going to tell your wife and son? ... They are going to say, you know, your father is a spy.

WEN HO LEE: But I, I'm not a spy—

FBI AGENT: ... What if they decide, okay. We're going to polygraph your wife?

WEN HO LEE: On what? On what subject?

FBI AGENT: What difference does it make? ... Your kids are going to have to live with this, okay. Your wife is going to have to live with it. This is going to eat away at them like a cancer. Just like the cancer that you had, but all the way ...

WEN HO LEE: Probably worse than the cancer.

FBI AGENT: That's right, it is worse than the cancer ...

WEN HO LEE: Well, okay, let's, let's stop here, 'cause I'm very tired ...

FBI AGENT: Wen Ho, this is serious ... Do you know who the Rosenbergs are?

WEN HO LEE: I heard then, yeah, I heard them mention.

FBI AGENT: The Rosenbergs are the only people that never cooperated with the federal government in an espionage case. You know what happened to them? They electrocuted them, Wen Ho.

WEN HO LEE: Yeah. I heard . . .

FBI AGENT: The Rosenbergs professed their innocence. The Rosenbergs weren't concerned either. The Rosenbergs are dead . . .

WEN HO LEE: Well, it . . . my life. I accept it, okay. I will try to do the best I can, and I, I believe, eventually . . . God. God, will make it his judge, judgment.

THE ANNOUNCER: Senator Peter Domenici, Republican of New Mexico:

SENATOR DOMENICI: That man [Wen Ho Lee] doesn't deserve civil liberties.

(Marcus, Leah and cast members, except for DHH, chant:)

PROTESTERS: Justice for Wen Ho Lee! Justice for Wen Ho Lee!

LEAH: I'm Asian American! Arrest me, too!

MARCUS: Racial Profile This!

PROTESTER #1: Asian American Does Not Equal Spy!

MARCUS: Who's next?

PROTESTERS: Who's next?

MARCUS: Who's next?

PROTESTERS: Who's next?

MARCUS: Who's next?

PROTESTERS: Who's next?

MARCUS: Who's next?

PROTESTERS: Who's next?

MARCUS: Who's next?

PROTESTERS: Who's next?

(The sounds of typing on two computer keyboards.)

DHH: So, Yellowgurl8, where are you *really* from?

YELLOWGURL8: Omaha. Growing up Vietnamese there, I felt so alone.

DHH: You're not alone.

YELLOWGURL8: I read your plays in high school.

DHH: Which ones?

(A phone rings. DHH does not pick up.)

YELLOWGURL8: All of them.
DHH: So—what are you wearing?

(DHH's machine picks up.)

DOROTHY HWANG: Dave, it's your mother. Just want to let you know. There's going to be an article tomorrow in the *New York Times*. About your father. It's a big one. Front page. And it's—it's not very good.
NWOAOC: *New York Times*, May 11, 1999: China sent cash to U.S. bank, with suspicions slow to rise. Written by—

(Sound cue: "Name Withheld on Advice of Counsel.")

NWOAOC: Late in the spring of 1996, federal bank examiners discovered that the central bank of China was moving tens of millions of dollars into the United States, depositing it in a maze of accounts ... at a small California bank ... Far East National ... *(Pause)* [Far East National's CEO, Henry Y.] Hwang, sixty-nine, is a well-known figure among Chinese Americans in Los Angeles ... [Hwang's] office is decorated with photographs of himself with various American presidents, including Bill Clinton, and with a poster from *M. Butterfly*, the Broadway hit written by his son, David Henry Hwang, who was formerly a director of the bank.
DHH: Oh shit.

(HYH, DHH and Dorothy Hwang.)

HYH: This reporter guy—no respect.
DHH: Dad—
HYH: Alice says, "Do you have an appointment?" This guy says, "No, I have to see Mr. Hwang." Then he just walks in! If I was in the bathroom, bet he'd just walk in there too. No class!
DHH: The first thing we gotta think about is—
HYH: You know, Son, I have a bathroom in my office—

DHH: I know.

HYH: With a shower and everything. Beautiful!

DOROTHY HWANG: Henry, listen to your son.

DHH: Dad! The newspaper article!

HYH: Right, right.

DOROTHY HWANG *(To DHH)*: Talk to your father.

HYH: Did you see the part when he called me "short"? I'm five-foot-ten! That's not short!

DHH: I know.

HYH: He called me short. You know what that means? The guy's a racist!

DHH: Dad! What's really important now, what you really have to worry about, is the senate investigation. Are you going to have to testify before Shelby's banking committee?

HYH: Of course!

DHH: You've already been subpoenaed?

HYH: Not yet. But I will be—no matter what it takes!

DHH: Wait, wait.

HYH: I told my lawyers—you spend whatever you have to, pull all the strings you've got—get me that subpoena!

DHH: You *want* to appear before the committee?

HYH: Of course!

DOROTHY HWANG: See, Dave? Why you have to talk to him?

HYH: On national television! Lights, cameras, senators—and me, giving it to those guys. "You—you discriminate against Asians! This sort of thing—must never happen in America."

DOROTHY HWANG: Dear, it's not going to go like that.

HYH: Ssssh! All around the country, people stop what they are doing, listen to me. And suddenly, the image of Asians is improved forever. Ah, beautiful!

DOROTHY HWANG: Dave?

DHH: Dad, it's very hard to make yourself look good before a congressional investigation.

HYH: What about Ollie North?

DHH: It's not impossible, but—

HYH: What does Ollie North have that I don't? First, I become a spokesman for Asians all around this country. Then next, who knows? Maybe—governor of California.

DOROTHY HWANG: Not again! He thinks he's going to become a hero.

HYH: This is my chance! To speak out for Asians in this country! Just like Marcus Gee!

DHH: That's not so easy!

HYH: This article—terrible! But the placement—very good! Front page of the *New York Times*! Dave, even you never been above the fold.

DHH: You really just wanna lie low and hope all this goes away. *(Cell phone rings. Pause)* Hang on.

HYH: Did you see my picture?

DHH: It's my cell phone.

HYH: I was wearing Armani!

DHH *(Into cell phone)*: Hello?

NWOAOC: May I speak to David Henry Hwang?

DHH: Speaking.

NWOAOC: My name is—

(Sound cue: "Name Withheld on Advice of Counsel.")

NWOAOC: I wrote the article in the *Times* this morning about Far East National.

DHH: Oh.

NWOAOC: I understand you were on Far East's board when all this occurred.

DHH: Well . . .

NWOAOC: I'd like the chance to prove you had nothing to do with this. If you wish, our talk could be completely off the record.

DHH: Um . . .

NWOAOC: So—can we meet?

(NWOAOC crosses to DHH, carrying a small tape recorder.)

(Regarding tape recorder): It's off.

DHH: Good. Because I don't think—

NWOAOC: I know. And I respect that.

DHH: So why—?

NWOAOC: Just in case *you* suddenly feel there's something *you* want to say on the record. It's here for your benefit. You control it. You just give the word. And it's ready to go.

DHH: You're not what I expected. I mean the way—

NWOAOC: The way I look?

DHH: Not that there's anything wrong with—

NWOAOC: I look like the guy who shows up to do your taxes, huh?

DHH: I don't really know what I was expecting, but—

NWOAOC: I suppose I should tell you about the first time I saw *M. Butterfly*. It was one of my most memorable evenings in the theater.

DHH: Thanks. That's very kind.

NWOAOC: To be honest, it's one of the reasons it kills me to see you mixed up in all this stuff. You don't need this. You don't wanna go before the Senate Banking Committee, believe me. The legal bills alone.

DHH: So why did you write the article?

NWOAOC: Can I tell you something about myself? I have no agenda. If I've gotten something wrong, I'm the first who's going to want to correct it. Because as a reporter, all I've got—my whole currency—is my reputation.

DHH: But what if there's no story here?

NWOAOC: Then that's what I'll write. David, I respect you a lot. I want to be corrected. Just give me a chance.

(Pause.)

DHH: All right. What do you want to know?

NWOAOC: You sat on the board of Far East National for quite a few years. Why?

DHH: Basically, as a favor to my father.

NWOAOC: Do you want to go on the record about this? You can go off at any moment—just by punching this button.

DHH: I can turn it off?

NWOAOC: Absolutely.

DHH: All right.

(NWOAOC turns on the tape recorder.)

When my father asked me, I was coming off one of the busiest years of my career. I turned him down at first.

NWOAOC: How did he convince you?

DHH: He said, "Son, I need your help." And, you know, growing up in a Chinese family, you feel an intense sense of duty to your parents. Filial piety is deeply ingrained in the culture. Dad took me to the grave of my Ti-Ti—my paternal grandfather—and there we lit joss sticks—incense. And it was as if the voices of my ancestors rose up, telling me it was my filial duty—to join the bank board. *(Pause)* Of course, I also felt a sense of responsibility to the Chinese American community.

NWOAOC: Can you explain?

DHH: Far East National served immigrants, refugees. I thought if I can help the bank succeed, it would help us all. As Chinese Americans, we need to empower ourselves—"By Any Means Necessary."

NWOAOC: This empowerment is important to you?

DHH: It's the reason for everything I do. Just a few years ago, for instance, I started to conquer a new world: network television, through which I'd be able to dig deep into the American psyche, dispelling stereotypes, creating positive images.

NWOAOC: Your television project—was it the Margaret Cho show?

(Pause. DHH turns off the tape recorder.)

DHH: I'd rather not talk about that, all right?

NWOAOC: You're the boss.

DHH: You know, I didn't write it. I was just brought in—to try and fix it.

NWOAOC: I understand. The whole subject. Gone. *(Regarding the tape recorder)* May I?

(Pause. NWOAOC turns the tape recorder back on.)

These large deposits from China—when they started rolling into the bank—were you aware of the size of these amounts?

DHH: You see, as a board member, I wasn't really all that concerned with the bank's finances.

NWOAOC: No?

DHH: I saw my role more as spiritual and moral compass.

NWOAOC: Could you explain that statement?

DHH: Well, you have to "fight the power."

NWOAOC: What power is that?

DHH: To put it bluntly, white America. We have to come together and marshal our collective resources to gain influence in this country.

NWOAOC: And so, from your position as a board member, you sought to use Far East's resources to gain influence—

DHH: Yes.

NWOAOC: For China.

DHH: No! I didn't say that.

NWOAOC: I'm sorry, I thought you did.

DHH: No, I was talking about gaining influence for Chinese Americans.

NWOAOC: Right.

DHH: Not China. There's a difference.

NWOAOC: But still—

DHH: What?

NWOAOC: Obviously if China becomes more powerful that strengthens the hand of the Chinese living here, wouldn't you agree?

DHH: No, I don't agree.

NWOAOC: You don't.

DHH: Listen, my loyalty is to America.

NWOAOC: But you just said you sought to "fight the power" of white America. Isn't that true?

(DHH reaches for the tape recorder.)

Before you punch that button, I think it's only fair to tell you that I've already gotten everything I need for my story. End this interview now, and you're not doing yourself any favors. Serious charges have been leveled against Far East National: money-laundering, violation of campaign finance laws, aiding a foreign power, possibly even complicity in espionage. As a bank director, you are legally and financially responsible for the activities under your watch. You look at me as if I'm your enemy. But I have no agenda. Which means I could be the best friend you've got in the world right now. Assuming you're innocent. Do I believe you solicited illegal deposits from China? Of course not! Do I believe you knew about the activity and turned a blind eye, at least in part to further the empowerment of your community? That's a more complicated question. But if you're innocent, I'm going to need more from you than the kind of spin you'd dish out to "Arts and Leisure." No, I'm going to need some real meat.

DHH: Look, I'm telling the truth. I knew practically nothing about the bank's dealings, really.

NWOAOC: I realize you were just Daddy's little rubber stamp. But that fact puts you in a position to enlighten me about something far more interesting than any balance sheet.

DHH: Like what?

NWOAOC: I want to know—about your father. How often does he go to China? Who does he see there? Has he ever expressed anger, bitterness, resentment towards America? Does he still have relatives in the old country? Friends? Anyone connected to the government? Or the military?

DHH: You're asking me—to give up my father.

NWOAOC: Only if there's something to give up. David, if there's one thing you care about, according to my research, it's what others think of you. I believe you're a loyal American. That's what I'd write about you. Just give me something to work with.

(Pause.)

DHH: Why are you going after my father?

NWOAOC: I'm reporting—on the work of federal investigators.

DHH: Who cleared him of this stuff—years ago.

NWOAOC: Well, now, they're reopening the case. Mr. Hwang, your father is a Chinese banker.

DHH: Chinese American.

NWOAOC: Exactly.

DHH: There's a difference.

NWOAOC: And it's that difference that interests me. If I were investigating Israeli espionage, I would look to the Jewish community—it's just logical. Does your father see himself as more American, or more Chinese?

DHH: That question makes no sense.

NWOAOC: On the contrary, I think it's quite relevant.

DHH: How about you? Do you see yourself as more American or more white?

NWOAOC: That's not the same thing.

DHH: No?

NWOAOC: Not in the least.

DHH: Why not?

NWOAOC: Because there's no conflict between being white and being American.

DHH: Did you really just say that? There's a conflict—between being Chinese and being American?

NWOAOC: No, of course I didn't mean—

DHH: And how convenient—we even got that on tape.

NWOAOC: I should've said it's not the same because white is a race, and China is a nation.

DHH: You should've, but you didn't. You know, you're going to make a fascinating character.

NWOAOC: What?

DHH: When I write a play about all this.

NWOAOC: You're going to write a play? About me?

DHH: I'm going to have to use that quote someplace.

NWOAOC: You can't.

DHH: Why not? You're writing about me, aren't you?

NWOAOC: I'm a reporter!

DHH: And I'm a playwright, nice to meet you. God, I really thought we were past all this: "yellow peril." "Where are you *really* from?"

NWOAOC: You are taking my slip completely out of context.

DHH: No, I'm putting it *in* context. According to *my* research, let's review your stories: the illegal sale of satellite technology to China, the campaign finance scandal, Wen Ho Lee, and, now, the charges against Far East National—they're all yours, aren't they?

NWOAOC: I wrote each one with a partner.

DHH: Oh, don't be modest. It's amazing to think one reporter has broken all those stories—that you managed to find so many evil Asians lurking in so many dark corners of this country. You look at folks like my dad—like Wen Ho Lee—and suddenly their eyes might as well be taped up and covered in piss-colored makeup. Cuz all you see are all those bad guys in the movies who ever put on yellow face.

NWOAOC: You have no idea what I do or don't see.

DHH: All right, then—as background research for my new show— *(Grabs tape recorder)* Would you care to explain—

why you see such a conflict between being Chinese and being American?

NWOAOC *(Takes back tape recorder)*: Mr. Hwang, there's ample evidence of illegal Chinese activity in this country. Your father received ninety-two million dollars in deposits from China. How do you explain that?

DHH: I'd say—he was successful.

NWOAOC: Obviously. But the money was funneled into a maze of accounts.

DHH: What—they're supposed to put ninety-two million dollars in one account?

NWOAOC: So you're going to sit there and tell me this entire investigation is completely baseless?

DHH: You know, you could've accused my dad of a half dozen other things and I would've gone, "Okay, well, maybe." But disloyalty to America? A country he loves, that's been his home for the last fifty years? How come, with Asians, the charge that always makes headlines is also the least original?

(NWOAOC turns off the tape recorder.)

NWOAOC: Okay, I gave you your chance.

DHH: I feel it's only fair to warn you—I already have everything I need to write my play.

NWOAOC: As if that's so difficult? Anything missing from your story—hell, you just go make it up.

DHH: Isn't that what all writers do?

NWOAOC: I search for a story to fit the facts, not the other way around.

DHH: But you arrange the facts, decide what's important and what's not—until you find a story that makes sense to your mind.

NWOAOC: You don't like my stories, fine, I present them as theories.

DHH: And I present mine as fiction. So what do you care if you end up in my play?

NWOAOC: I'm no one! There's nothing about me in the media. I've kept it that way. You see, Mr. Hwang, I'm anonymous.

DHH: All the more reason for me to start writing. You really deserve a little more attention for your impressive body of work. You broke Whitewater, too, didn't you? And wasn't *that* a great service to this country?

NWOAOC: Just understand this: if you use my real name, you will find yourself in court. The *Times* is quite vigilant in matters like these.

DHH: You can't sue me if this conversation actually happened.

NWOAOC: As far as I'm concerned, it didn't.

DHH: But there's a tape.

NWOAOC: What tape?

DHH: No? So how will you write your story on me?

NWOAOC: I won't. Fortunately, you didn't provide any useful information for my research.

DHH: Funny. Cuz you provided plenty for my play.

NWOAOC: Sorry you can't use my name. But, hey, you can always use your own.

DHH: Don't be ridiculous. When you write an autobiographical play, no one uses their real name. That would be self-indulgent.

NWOAOC: You talk like someone who's actually written a play in ages.

DHH: Well, thank you. For giving me something to say again.

NWOAOC: Have a good time before the Senate Banking Committee. It's an experience, believe me. Maybe you can write about it.

(NWOAOC ends the scene.)

OCC: Office of the Comptroller of the Currency. [To Henry Y. Hwang: Your] application for a charter to organize a new federal bank is denied.

OCC REGIONAL DIRECTOR: We couldn't give Henry Hwang another bank charter. Not . . . while he was under investigation. Approval [by us, at that time] . . . would have invited serious congressional scrutiny.

DR. PICHORAK: David, we still have more treatment options available for your father. But so far, his cancer markers are not going down, and the PET scan suggests the condition may have metastasized to his liver. Honestly, we caught that first tumor so early—the chemo should've knocked it right out. But it seems your father's case is—particularly aggressive.

(DHH crosses to HYH.)

DHH: Listen, Dad—Mom found this new gene-therapy treatment. It's experimental, but we think we can get you into the
clinical—

HYH: Wait. You know, Son, I used to believe in America, but
now, I don't anymore. I don't even put my money into
minority banks anymore, because the system doesn't play
fair. I put my money into mainstream banks, where at least
it will be safe. *(Pause)* When I was a kid in Shanghai, my
favorite star of all was Jimmy Stewart. He was so kind,
always doing things for other people. And when the chips
were down, he would give it to the bad guys, tell them off,
and everyone would listen to him. When I started the bank,
I thought, Now, I can be Jimmy Stewart, too. But when I try
to stop those guys who are after me, I can't beat them this
time. I'm not Jimmy Stewart after all. *(Pause)* So, Dave,
I don't want any new fancy treatment. My real life—it's not
here anymore. I'm ready to go. And I'll do it my way.

(DHH leaves HYH. Marcus crosses to DHH.)

MARCUS: David? I heard about your father's illness. And if
there's anything I can do to help, anything at all—

DHH: Why are you torturing me?! Why won't you leave me
alone? Get out of my life? Why do you keep popping up—
every place I look—being all good and noble and completely disgusting?

MARCUS: Well, er, thanks for the compliment.

DHH: Why do you do all this?

MARCUS: Cuz it feels good. To be part of something—bigger than
myself. *(Pause)* How's your dad?

DHH: Hanging around the ICU, career in tatters, trying to sur-
vive an American purge—other than that, he's great.

MARCUS: I read that story about him in the *Times*.

DHH: You and the rest of the world. It's all gotten too big, too
many investigations. They've gotta bag some game, or else
end up looking really bad. That's all Dad needs—to finish his
life in prison.

MARCUS: What can we do to help him?

DHH: You can help me—by going away.

MARCUS: Sorry, I was just trying to—

DHH: Yeah, well, it's easy. For you to "help." You're holding all the cards.

MARCUS: I'm under investigation, too, remember?

DHH: And all you'd have to do to save yourself—is take off your mask. Let them know who you really are.

MARCUS: You think I don't know that? Sure, I could save myself. But what good would that do the community? The investigators would hush up my case, and keep going after people like your dad.

DHH: Unless—

MARCUS: What?

DHH: Unless they couldn't.

MARCUS: Couldn't what?

DHH: I mean, unless they couldn't hush it up.

MARCUS: I don't—

DHH: Listen. You really want to help the community?

MARCUS: Yes, but—

DHH: Then take off your mask. Not behind closed doors, or on some little cell phone call. No, do it in public. Where the bastards won't be able to make you go away. Can you imagine? How idiotic all their investigations will look? Once the American public learns that in their determination to find evil Chinese spies, this government spent millions of taxpayer dollars—just to end up going after . . . a regular American?

MARCUS: You want me to talk to the press? But if I go public with who I really am—I'll have to leave the community. I mean, people will be so pissed, they'll never accept me again. And, David, I love this community!

DHH: How much? More than yourself?

MARCUS: You're talking about my whole life! And, you know, it wouldn't be just me who'd get into trouble, it'd be you, too.

DHH: What do you—?

MARCUS: How could I come out as white—without explaining how I got mistaken as Asian?

DHH: Good point.

MARCUS: So we agree.

DHH: All right, then I'll go with you to the interview. Explain how this whole misunderstanding came about. That you'd never have been able to pass yourself off as an Asian except for me. That it was all my fault.

MARCUS: You would do that? *(Pause)* You know, it'll make you look bad.

DHH: Marcus, do you remember the Chinese concept of "face"?

MARCUS: Yeah, but why are you—?

DHH: I'm willing to go out there and lose my face. How 'bout you?

NWOAOC: *New York Times*: staffers probing Chinese investigations cast too wide a net. Written by . . . me. Officials probing accusations of illegal campaign contributions from Chinese donors are investigating a U.S. citizen with—

LEAH *(Overlapping)*: —with no Asian ancestry at all. *(To Marcus)* I'm reading this in the paper. So it can't possibly be true. Right?

MARCUS: Leah, please. Nothing's really changed about me. Just my past, right?

LEAH: I see. Yes, right. Which means, everything's changed about you, Marcus. Did you ever tell me the truth? About anything?

MARCUS: Leah, I love you—that was never a lie. You gotta believe me.

LEAH: I do. And believing you—makes me sick to my stomach. *(Pause)* Don't touch me! *(Exits the play)*

NWOAOC: The origins of this almost comical mishap involve a strange cast of characters, including Tony Award–winning playwright, David Henry Hwang.

DHH: I cast Marcus as an Asian in my play, not knowing he was actually a white man. After I realized my mistake, I tried to conceal my blunder by passing him off as a—Siberian Jew.

NWOAOC *(To the audience)*: How could I resist a story like that? It was just too delicious. *(Pause)* You see? I told the truth. I really have no agenda. *(Exits the play)*

DHH: After the *Times* ran its story unmasking Marcus, Jay Leno joked in his monologue that federal investigators were now planning to go after Pamela and Tommy Lee, Neil Sedaka, and the lead singer from Wang Chung. This marked the turning point in the Chinese espionage scandals of the late 1990s. Shelby's banking committee ended their investigation, without ever subpoenaing my father. Fred Thompson's probe withered away. Wen Ho Lee spent nine months in solitary confinement before the charges against him were finally dropped by Judge James Parker.

JUDGE JAMES PARKER: I sincerely apologize to you, Dr. Lee, for the unfair manner you were held in captivity . . . which has embarrassed our nation and all of its citizens. *(Exits the play)*

ROCCO: Rocco Palmieri, former aide to Senator Fred Thompson, posting on realclearpolitics.com. So. The Chinese won the first round. But we were on the right track. 9/11 threw this country into an extended distraction phase. Once Osama bin Laden and his cronies have been brought under control, this country will wake up and realize—while we've been expending our time and resources in the Middle East, our real enemies have been taking advantage of this window to make themselves even more formidable. The Chinese investigations aren't over, not by a long shot. They're merely on hiatus until our next war begins—because America's real enemy in the twenty-first century—will be China. *(Exits the play)*

HYH: *New York Times*, October 13, 2005: Henry Y. Hwang, who founded the first Asian American–owned federally chartered bank in the Continental United States, died Saturday at his home in San Marino, California. He was seventy-seven. *(Exits the play)*

DHH: My father's obituary was picked up by the wire services, and ran in over two hundred and fifty media outlets, from Mississippi to Taiwan. I thought he would've liked that. *(Pause)* Marcus came to my father's memorial service. Afterwards, we went for a walk. *(To Marcus)* I always kind of believed Dad would be able to talk his way out of anything. He was the only person I'd ever known who went in for an IRS audit and came out with a bigger refund.

MARCUS: I see your point.

DHH: I can't believe he's really gone.

MARCUS: I'm sorry.

DHH: But here's the part that gets me. In the end, he even lost his dream—and you know something? Maybe that's what really killed him. Sick as I got of hearing his shtick, it had been Dad's whole life: his faith that in America, you can imagine who you want to be—and, through sheer will and determination, become that person. *(Pause)* If only it were true.

MARCUS: But it is. Look at me.

DHH: Huh?

MARCUS: I imagined myself as something completely different from what I was—

DHH: No, no, no, no.

MARCUS: And then, through sheer will and determination, just like your dad—

DHH: I can't believe you're going there. Listen, you are nobody's idea of the American Dream, okay?

MARCUS: Then why did you create me?

(Pause.)

DHH: Uh, Marcus?

MARCUS: Be honest. I'm a character. In this play you've written about your dad, and yourself, and what happened with that, that reporter who we're not supposed to say his real name.

DHH: I . . . wasn't planning to get into this.

MARCUS: I think you should.

DHH: No, see, I was planning to maintain the ambiguity about reality versus fiction—through the end of the play.

MARCUS: Well, I think that's intellectually dishonest.

DHH: Hey, hey! If you're my creation, do what I say!

MARCUS: C'mon, Dave—any characters worth their salt eventually go their own way. Now tell the truth. You can do it.

DHH: This is . . . kind of humiliating.

MARCUS: It's a little late in the show to start worrying about humiliating yourself.

DHH *(To the audience)*: Marcus is . . . a fictional character. Created by me.

MARCUS: Why?

DHH: Because . . . I'm a writer. And, in the end, everything's always all about me.

MARCUS: And?

DHH: Okay. Years ago, I discovered a face—one I could live better and more fully than anything I'd ever tried. But as the years went by, my face became my mask. And I became just another actor—running around in yellow face. *(Pause)* That's where you came in. To take words like "Asian" and "American," like "race" and "nation," mess them up so bad no one has any idea what they even mean anymore. Cuz that was Dad's dream: a world where he could be Jimmy Stewart. And a white guy—can even be an Asian. *(Pause)* That's what you do after your father dies. You start making his dream your own.

MARCUS: And now, you don't need me anymore. *(Pause)* But do me a favor. Write me a happy ending, okay?

DHH: They're not my specialty . . . but I'll try. I'll send you to a Chinese village—called Zhencong. *(To the audience)* Final e-mail. From Marcus G. Dahlman to David Henry Hwang. Received . . . sometime tomorrow.

(Dong Track #2: "We Close the Village for Rituals." Marcus appears in a separate space from DHH.)

MARCUS: Dear David, It's happened at last. Nine months after my arrival in Dong country. Tonight, as they gathered together for the "big song," I saw a couple of villagers gesturing for me to come closer. I got up, and ascended the steps under the eaves to the pagoda. And no one stopped me. They saw who I am, and gave me "face." As I opened my mouth, the music began to speak to me, in words only I could hear:

> Get over yourself.
> This song is only doing
> What it has always done:
> Taking in voices
> From all the lands
> And all the peoples,
> Who have ever crossed its path.
> Though that road has been messy,
> It made this song.
> For nothing of value,
> Nothing which lasts,
> Nothing human,
> Is ever pure.

(Pause.)

I joined the "big song," and found the thing I had lost. A reason to hope. And now, I can go home.

(Music out.)

DHH *(To the audience)*: Hey, it could happen. For Marcus, the play ends. And I go back to work, searching for my own face.

(Lights fade to black.)

END OF PLAY

DAVID HENRY HWANG is the author of *M. Butterfly* (1988 Tony, Drama Desk, Outer Critics Circle awards; Pulitzer Prize finalist), *Golden Child* (1998 Tony nomination; 1997 OBIE Award), *FOB* (1981 OBIE Award), *The Dance and the Railroad* (1982 Drama Desk nomination), *Family Devotions* (1982 Drama Desk nomination), *Sound and Beauty* and *Bondage*. He wrote the books for the Broadway musicals *Aida* (co-author), *Flower Drum Song* (2002 revival; 2003 Tony nomination) and Disney's *Tarzan*. His opera libretti include three works for composer Philip Glass, *1000 Airplanes on the Roof*, *The Voyage* (The Metropolitan Opera) and *The Sound of a Voice*, as well as Bright Sheng's *The Silver River*, Osvaldo Golijov's *Ainadamar* (two 2007 Grammy awards), Unsuk Chin's *Alice in Wonderland* (Opernwelt's 2007 world premiere of the year) and Howard Shore's *The Fly*. Hwang penned the feature films *M. Butterfly*, *Golden Gate* and *Possession* (co-author). He also co-wrote the song "Solo" with Prince. He attended Stanford University and the Yale School of Drama, and was appointed by President Clinton to the President's Committee on the Arts and the Humanities. He serves on the council of the Dramatists Guild of America.

Yellow Face received a 2008 OBIE Award for Playwriting and it was a finalist for the 2008 Pulitzer Prize.